I0065413

forces at work

forces at work

How to Get What You Want and Keep What You Value

MISSY SHOPSHIRE

Niche Pressworks

FORCES AT WORK

ISBN-13:   Paperback   978-1-952654-80-0
　　　　　 Hardback   978-1-952654-79-4
　　　　　 eBook   978-1-952654-81-7

Copyright © 2023 by Missy Shopshire

All rights reserved. No part of this book may be used or reproduced in any manner whatsoever without prior written consent of the author, except as provided by the United States of America copyright law.

Scriptures marked "ESV" are taken from the ESV® Bible (The Holy Bible, English Standard Version®), copyright © 2001 by Crossway, a publishing ministry of Good News Publishers. Used by permission. All rights reserved. The ESV text may not be quoted in any publication made available to the public by a Creative Commons license. The ESV may not be translated in whole or in part into any other language.

The author of this book does not dispense medical advice or prescribe the use of any technique as a form of treatment for physical, emotional, or medical problems, either directly or indirectly. The intent of the author is only to offer information of a general nature to help you in your quest for emotional, physical, and spiritual well-being. In the event you use any of the information in this book for yourself, the author and the publisher assume no responsibility for your actions.

To protect the privacy of others, certain names and details have been changed. For permission to reprint portions of this content or for bulk purchases, contact missy@missyshopshire.com.

Published by Niche Pressworks; NichePressworks.com, Indianapolis, IN.

Cover photography by Lori Cardwell.

The views expressed herein are solely those of the author and do not necessarily reflect the views of the publisher.

dedication

For Lindy and all who loved her.
She was a Force at Work

contents

foreword by **Bob Goff**

I met Missy when she attended a conference where I was speaking about my first book, *Love Does*. My message resonated with her, so she stayed connected with what I was doing and most recently participated in the first School of Whimsey I held in Anaheim, California. I created the School of Whimsey to help others dream big and take bold actions as they grow and share their gifts with the world.

It was there that Missy told me about her dream to write *Forces at Work*, and she boldly asked me if I would consider writing the Foreword for it. I said yes! So here we are.

Forces at Work is a love letter for anyone who feels stuck, pigeonholed, or misaligned in their life or career. If you are looking for theory, you won't find it here. What you will find is deep empathy and a framework for clarity based on Missy's hard-won life lessons. You'll be gently guided by the skill and experience of a gifted coach who meets you where you are and helps you reflect and take action to realign your life with purpose.

Missy has already helped hundreds of people find the courage and conviction to step into their highest aspirations. I know this book will help her reach many more. Because, just like me, she is in love with your potential, and together, all of us are Forces at Work!

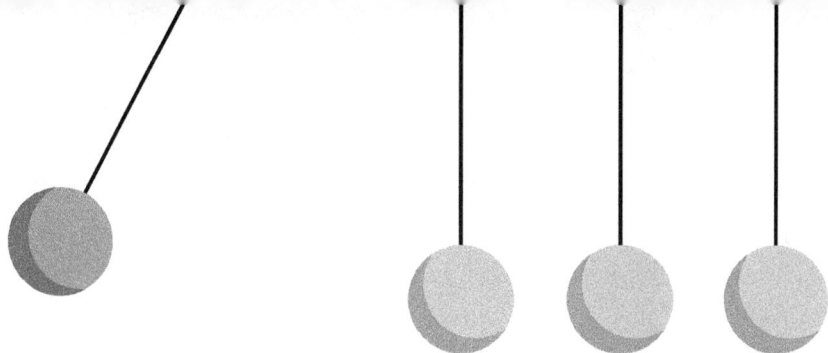

awaken the forces within

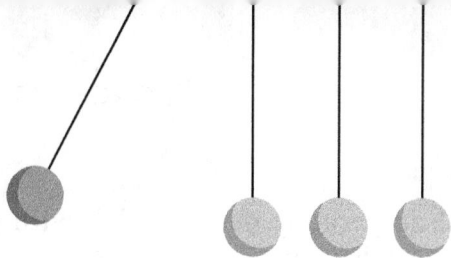

CHAPTER 1

waking up

"Some of us get woken up by the harsh realities of life. We suffer so much that we wake up. Other people keep bumping into life again and again. They still go on sleepwalking. They never wake up."

— Anthony De Mello

Two days after giving birth to our youngest child, unforeseen complications landed me in a medically induced coma. I was not expected to live.

Pre-coma, I ranked in the top 2 percent of all consultants in a multi-billion-dollar sales organization representing the number-one brand of skincare and color cosmetics in America. I had a wonderful husband and three healthy children. I had acquired all the trappings of success — a beautiful home, a luxury company car, and great vacations.

The problem was, I kept having to remind myself that things were great.

I almost always wore a smile and had a positive outlook on life. I had stumbled into this sales career at a time when

I desperately needed a job with good income potential and flexibility. Driven by our financial needs, I hadn't stopped to consider whether it was a good fit for me or fulfilled a deeper purpose in my life.

If I was good at *it*, how could it not be good for *me*?

I assumed I had found "success" because I knew how to increase my revenue year over year. But I was working on autopilot. I often wondered if I was living up to my potential. I certainly wasn't enjoying my life as much as my Facebook page would have led you to believe (#blessed). But I didn't want to complain, so I focused on being grateful.

I knew I had much more to be grateful for than just the flexibility and cash flow my career provided. The year before my illness, our four-year-old daughter had won a hard-fought battle with stage 3 kidney cancer. When it rains, it pours.

During our respective health challenges, I couldn't have asked for a more supportive team. My sales directors and consultants showed up for me in every possible way — helping with the kids, taking care of my clients, and bringing meals. I was overwhelmed by the love shown to my family. And yet, it didn't ease my restlessness.

As I started down the long road to my physical recovery, I couldn't shake the feeling — or maybe the wishful longing — that I was meant for something else.

Slowing Down

These physical challenges had unseen benefits (and not just because the members of Grace Community Church brought cheesy casseroles to my door for almost two years straight).

First, my daughter's illness forced me to slow down long enough for my thoughts to catch up with me, and then my own health crisis stopped me in my tracks completely. In both cases, I faced unimaginable fear: first, the fear of losing my child, and then the fear of my own death. Fear pushed in, landing front and center in my life. It wanted to call the shots, to keep me small and tether me to the safest path.

Walking closely with fear opened my eyes to the other ways it had intruded into my life. I had let it compromise my dreams and influence my decisions. I suppose fear is never a welcome companion, but as we became better acquainted, it offered me two precious gifts. It woke me to what really mattered to me, and it made me recognize and retire my passive acceptance of my life and work.

While I was unconscious, sepsis had ravaged my body, literally leaving me with a broken heart. I woke up feeling weak and powerless. In a blink, this near-death experience had stolen my perfect health and replaced it with a chronic heart condition.

My heart was struggling to beat at less than 30 percent of its normal capacity. Doctors told me I had developed cardiomyopathy and congestive heart failure. They warned that my life would look very different going forward. They were right, but thankfully not because of the condition of my physical heart. It has since healed completely.

Instead, my life looks different because this coma-inducing illness was a severe mercy — a divine intervention that jarred me awake and forced me to accept an unavoidable reality: I have one precious life to live.

Four days later, I regained consciousness. I woke trembling with gratitude. It filled me up and spilled out of me. I was so lucky to be alive! All my senses were heightened.

Colors appeared brighter; music brought me to tears; the faces of my family overwhelmed me with love. I had an undefined but unquenchable desire for my life to matter.

I was internally determined to heal my physical heart. For several months, I took ridiculously good care of myself. I enjoyed long, unhurried talks with my closest friends and family. I slept at least eight hours a night, ate healthy food, and eventually started working out again. Nurturing my body awakened my soul. A door to a new life was opening before me — not a perfect life, but a more authentic, purposeful, and extraordinary one.

I became keenly aware that I had some decisions to make.

The first was what to do with my role as a sales consultant and director — a role that was currently paying the bills and supporting our lifestyle. Though I loved the company and the women who surrounded me, I didn't enjoy selling makeup or mustering enthusiasm over the perfect shade of foundation or the shimmer in an eye shadow. I wanted more meaning and less hustle. I wanted to find my purpose.

Chasing Purpose

I dabbled with finding my purpose by taking assessments and attending webinars here and there. Even though they helped me gather some interesting information about myself, none of it seemed actionable, and I could never see beyond the big wall of what felt realistic. So, I hired a life coach.

Coaching was powerful. It wasn't long before I started to believe not only that I had a unique and important purpose but also that I could use it to create the life I wanted. Intrigued and impressed by this powerful transformative process called coaching, I decided to become a certified and credentialed life coach myself. As I found my own way, I eagerly shared what I was learning with my team. Then I began sharing it with other executives, entrepreneurs, coaches, and consultants. Eventually, I left my career in sales and started coaching full-time.

Navigating purpose on our own is like sailing a wide ocean of possibility in a tiny boat with no compass or map to guide us. An extraordinary adventure lies ahead, but how can we know if we have enough energy and resources to find it? As the sun burns hot and the day draws on without discovering a new shore, we are forced to paddle back to our familiar island. Collaborating with a coach is like having a map and a guide with us through the treacherous waters of uncertainty.

Without a working understanding of our purpose, we are baffled by our own behavior. We waffle over decisions. Everything feels harder than it should. We wonder: How can we feel bored and exhausted at the same time? And without a meaningful purpose to ground us, we become susceptible to fruitless distractions and addictive behaviors. Our best efforts and good intentions seem only to frame us into a role or a career we no longer love — or maybe never loved at all. All of this further dims our belief that change is possible. Having parked our potential in a garage far away, we rarely speak about our passions and dreams. Instead, we numb the pain of misalignment with endless entertainment and Kardashian-infused Kool-Aid. We argue for our own limitations and hear ourselves say things like:

"That ship has sailed."
"It's too late to change."
"I made my bed, and now I need to lie in it."
"I should just be grateful."

And the worst one of all, "This is just the way things are."
We keep climbing the corporate ladder because this is what successful people do. Even if others applaud our work ethic, we compare ourselves with co-workers or neighbors and come up lacking. Endlessly scrolling through social media, we wonder if we are measuring up. Comparison leaves us feeling empty and lost. We have become vogue on the outside but vague on the inside.

In the meantime, we may be missing our real work — our unique and important contribution that will ignite our souls and positively impact the

> We have become vogue on the outside but vague on the inside.

world. Children in underdeveloped countries are waiting for food and lifesaving surgeries. Vulnerable kids in our own foster care system are experiencing trauma and neglect. A confused and angry teenager is taking a gun to school. Underfunded arts programs leave our future creatives without mentors or direction. Our own families lack the time and connection they need to feel loved, supported, and nurtured. Our planet heaves under the weight of exploitation, and our political system has become a circus.

We lament these realities on our social media pages. We wish we could do more, and we might have even identified a specific cause in which we want to become involved... someday. Because, for all our stunning professional achievements, we are surprisingly hesitant when it comes to actively embracing what really matters to us on a deeper level.

Like tired sailors rowing a small boat, we assume more arduous work is required. We don't notice that a beautiful vessel carrying our purpose is docked at the shore, its sails waiting to unfurl, catch the wind, and carry us far beyond the horizon we see today.

So, we grab another glass of wine and commiserate with the other unfulfilled souls around us, settling further into our belief that this must be as good as life gets.

But if we listen carefully, we'll hear our soul whisper that there is more for us. And if we trust this voice, we can find our way.

Your Ship Has Not Sailed: It Is Waiting for You

I don't believe your ship has sailed. It is still there, docked and waiting.

And your wild hope is real, too, though sometimes you don't want to let yourself believe it. You can attain the life you dare to dream of.

You can become a Force at Work.

Forces at Work are extraordinary, open-hearted, compelling leaders who know who they are and what they bring to the world. They are confident and secure in their ability to start and finish work that matters to them — and they intuitively recognize that their work is much more than where they spend the hours from eight to five. Their greatest work is investing their precious, limited personal energy to make a difference in their lives and in the lives of others. Though they are well acquainted with success, they resist complacency and are first in line when an opportunity to learn or grow arises.

Becoming a Force at Work is about becoming the truest, most authentic, empowered version of yourself. Forces at Work are connected to a higher power, and they believe they serve a purpose that is larger than themselves. They have a big appetite for life. They operate as if pleasure and purpose are intricately entwined and are waiting to be discovered and rediscovered as the seasons of life change. Forces at Work respect themselves and their abilities, and they enjoy rich, collaborative relationships with others.

Sadly, many of us are not experiencing this kind of life. We have gotten stuck somewhere along the path by making compromises we thought were necessary. Like unrelenting weeds in a beautiful garden, work, stress, and other people's expectations strangle our joy and limit our growth. We confuse service with sacrifice and martyr ourselves beyond recognition. We point to our past successes and keep mailing it in, but we are emotionally disconnected from our souls. Abandoning our vision requires us to choose limiting beliefs about ourselves and others. These beliefs are as real as steel bars, and they trap us in a status quo prison of our own making. Being stuck at a high level still feels stuck.

Fortunately, the answer is simple and available to all of us: Awaken the Forces within. This book delivers an empowered approach to living by aligning five powerful elements: Purpose, Vision, Agency, Intention, and Action — the Forces at Work within us. Through this process, you can restore integrity with yourself and begin to unravel your limiting beliefs and excuses that keep you from reaching your highest goals and aspirations.

I want you to know I am not sitting in an ivory tower eating bonbons as if I have figured this all out. I am a compassionate coach who will walk with you as you pull back the curtain on your **purpose** and illuminate the **vision** that already lives inside you. I will lend you my belief in what is possible. I'll ask the right questions, and I'll share stories of my clients and others who have walked this path and whose lives are forever changed in remarkable and amazing ways.

I'll offer an overview of these five elements that help us find our way. In addition to **purpose** and **vision**, I will help you restore your sense of **agency** and teach you the power of your own **intentions.** I will challenge you to create **inspired actions** that transform you and lead to your most meaningful work and contribution to the world.

You can enjoy an extraordinary and adventurous life while serving others in a way that matters — and in a way that only you can. In fact, I believe you are reading this book because you possess a unique and important purpose that is ready to be unveiled.

Not only that, but you won't have to work so hard.

Because the good news is that finding alignment in our lives doesn't require working harder or doing more. (It usually requires doing less!) Through this book, I'd like to be your personal coach. There is a free *Forces at Work Guidebook* available on my website to help you process every chapter. You might want to grab yours now. Both the guidebook and these chapters were written to support and celebrate the

Force at Work you are becoming. Your part is to keep reading, trust the process, and take your next right step by answering the reflection questions after each chapter.

So, I have one question. Are you ready to wake up?

Reflection

What drew you to read *Forces at Work*? Do you ever find yourself wondering if this is as good as life gets? What are you hoping to find in these pages?

RESOURCES FOR THE FORCES

My vision for Forces at Work goes way beyond these pages. Below are some ways you can expand your experience and connect with other Forces at Work while you read.

ForcesAtWork.com
You will want to head over to forcesatwork.com to download the free *Forces at Work Guidebook* that accompanies this book. There, you'll also find fun swag, retreat information, and other ways to connect with me.

#ForcesAtWork
Share your insights, practices, and projects while you read using #forcesatwork on Twitter or Instagram. (I'm @MissyShopshire)

Forces at Work Spotify Soundtrack
Listen to the Forces at Work Playlist while you read! Search for "Forces at Work" by Missy Shopshire, or just listen to anything by the most inspirational artist of all time, Andy Grammar (shameless fan plug, I know).

Join the Force
Join the free Forces at Work community! Receive monthly encouragement and membership access to the private Facebook circle and be the first to learn about upcoming opportunities. Join at forcesatwork.com.

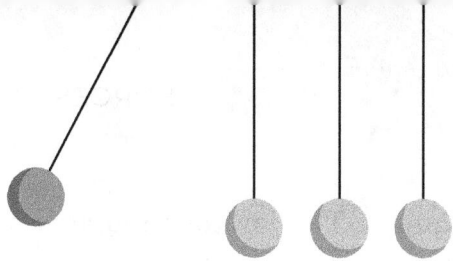

CHAPTER 2

unpause
your potential

I hope you live a life you're proud of. If you find that you are not,
I hope you have the strength to start all over again.

— F. Scott Fitzgerald

knew Steven was special the first time I met him. Recently hired to be the music director at our church, he had a raw musical talent. He captivated his audience, and he brought incredible energy and creativity to his work. Effortlessly flying from the piano to the guitar and bringing out the best from every performer on the stage with him, he was a breath of fresh air for our congregation. Authentic and vulnerable, he wove the best and hardest parts of life into the music he shared with us each week. He quickly became known as a caring leader for the arts community in our congregation.

His wife, Amanda, is also incredibly talented and often shared the stage with him, singing and playing the electric guitar. The joy they radiated as they performed together was contagious. They were also parents, raising two beautiful little girls.

Mega churches place a lot of emphasis on a big service every weekend. Steven and Amanda never disappointed. In quiet moments, they made the large space feel small, sacred, and intimate, allowing for reflection and stillness. When celebrating, they had the crowd roaring with power and energy. Experts at reading the room and guiding the mood, they effortlessly prepared hearts to receive the pastor's message each week.

We got to know each other through a small group and became good friends. I was a little surprised when Steven confided that he was really struggling with his role. Curious and wondering if I could help, I invited him for some coaching. He eagerly accepted.

When he came to my office, I was stunned to learn how truly unhappy he had been feeling. The downcast, dejected person in my office contrasted with the brilliant performer I saw on stage each week.

As we explored his situation, he shared that he felt trapped. While he loved the stage time and the creative opportunities his role provided, Steven also had a big vision and a desire to make a greater contribution as a strategic leader. He felt he had been clear about this during the interview process but that the church leadership had quickly relegated him to being "the music guy."

Throughout the week, he attended endless meetings in which he was asked to support initiatives but not to contribute to their development. Steven wanted to be a team player but often felt shut down when he offered his perspective, so he eventually stopped raising his hand.

"They are looking for followers, not leaders," he said, clearly frustrated.

He went on, sharing how going along with decisions was getting harder and harder. He felt like a puppet. Navigating the disparity between how he was feeling and how he had to show up to perform required mental gymnastics and effort to pull off. He had started to believe maybe this was just the way things were and that he should expect such compromises like this in any job.

Worse, all of this had him feeling out of integrity with himself. The church paid a moderate salary and provided health insurance for his family. Knowing what struggling as an artist was like, Steven feared leaving and being unable to support his family. He didn't know what else to do.

The only option he saw was to make the best of it and manage his frustration as best as he could.

Over the last 15 years, I've seen this happen to people in almost every imaginable profession. I've worked with doctors, lawyers, surgeons, CEOs, artists, financial planners, non-profit directors, and product managers. Most of them look as if they have achieved success. They believe they should feel happy. But for some reason, they don't.

Blown off Track

As competent and capable leaders, we can easily become misaligned with our true purpose when we say yes and jump in whenever we see a need or when others call upon us to lead. Whether it is a job or another cause we care about, we start in good faith and hope for the best. We want to serve others, and we feel a moral obligation to "do the right thing." We invest our time, energy, and effort, hoping to get to a place where it finally feels worth it. Even if we have climbed to the top of the pile and planted our flag, we look around and see we don't have the life or relationships we really wanted. What's worse is that we don't know who we are anymore.

I hear this story from executives and entrepreneurs alike who feel frustrated at being cast in roles they no longer want to play. Every year that goes by is a passive investment in a life that feels out of sync, another brick in the wall that seems determined to block out any light from the other side of a decision they made years ago. They also feel pressured to stop complaining and be grateful. No one wants to be the fated dog who looked into the water and let go of the bone in his mouth to grab the illusory one he thought he saw in his reflection.

What do you do when you've invested everything in getting what you want and then discover it's not what you want anymore? How do you change what feels set in concrete when you've built the rest of your life on top of it? How do you break loose from the personality you've created based on this performance when the people you love are depending on you to play your role and keep the show going? How do you unpause your potential and allow yourself to dream again?

For the next six months, Steven came to my office every other week, and I shared the same coaching principles with him that I'm about to share with you now. We had transformational conversations around five key areas of his life, and each week he would act on our conversation.

We didn't focus on fixing his job or on finding a new one. We had a bigger goal.

Looking Inward Vs. Outward

If we had focused on the external issues at hand, Steven might have made a lateral move and landed in a similar role. In fact, he did make several pitstops while getting to where he is now. Ultimately, Steven recognized that he had untapped potential, and he could dream bigger. By looking inside, he discovered unlimited options available to him and believed he could succeed wherever and however he chose to employ his talents and passions.

Steven had an external battle going on with the church leadership, but more importantly, he was at war with himself. The leader and artist who wanted to express himself was fighting with the young husband and father who wanted to provide for his family.

When we feel stuck and frustrated, it is as if we are trying to read the label from inside the jar. My job as coach was to help him read the parts of the label he was struggling to see. The external issues would resolve when he uncovered his purpose. Once we established his guiding purpose, Steven was able to take the next steps to align his vision, agency, intention, and action in service of fulfilling it.

Transformation Is Possible

Today, Steven is a professor and director of music studies at Samford University. He also runs Hereafter Music Studios, where he has collaborated with such musicians as James Taylor, The Band Perry, Josh Garrels, and many other prolific artists of our time. He recently called to tell me CBS picked up one of his original pieces for a sitcom.

Steven is a Force at Work. He serves others without martyring himself. He still faces challenges but no longer feels oppressed. He knows who he is, how he wants to show up in the world, and what he wants to contribute. His success has led to many opportunities, and by operating in powerful alignment, he recognizes the projects that are for him and confidently declines those that are not.

We celebrated the offer he received from CBS not just for the external validation and the revenue it will bring but because this work is an extension of who he is and the truest expression of the unique gifts and influence he wants to share with the world.

I know Steven has a big purpose in the world. If you are reading this book, I believe you do, too. I am on a mission to change the world by helping extraordinary leaders like you embrace their highest aspirations for their lives and their careers.

The Two Great Forces at Work: Fear and Love

Love is the only thing stronger than whatever is wrong with us.
— *Earnie Larsen*

If you are feeling misaligned, trapped, or like you haven't fully explored your potential, keep reading. If you have invested in your education, gained experience, and worked hard to achieve success in your given field, and yet found the destination not all you hoped for, you will find a way forward in these pages.

But first and foremost, we must establish one important fact. Forces at Work is about shifting your energy from fear to love.

Fear and love are the two great universal Forces at Work in each of us. How you navigate them will determine the course of your life.

> Forces at Work is about shifting your energy from fear to love.

Fear makes you feel desperate and keeps you in step. Fear shuts out the voice of purpose and suggests a safer program instead. Fear shows you how to fit in and hide like a chameleon when your true colors might draw too much attention and make those around you uncomfortable. When abundance surrounds you, fear tells you to hoard and hang on tightly to what is yours. Fear has you build your own small kingdom and keeps you circling inside the gates while looking outside yourself for validation and acceptance. Fear says you must constantly prove your worth, and it torments you when you stop for rest.

The force that sets us free is love. Love whispers that you are OK and you are here to grow and to learn. Love knows your unique, important purpose and calls you to step into your highest aspirations for your life and your career. Love holds both your achievements and your failures loosely, separately from your worth, and invites you to operate from a place of abundance and acceptance. Love ignites your imagination and inspires you to dream of a better world. And love awakens your deepest desires, encouraging you to follow them and uncover the treasure of your purpose.

To align your life with purpose, you will first need to commit to the internal journey from fear to love. This journey requires you to recognize when fear is interfering with your best thoughts and to uncover any fear that might be hiding under anger, sadness, or apathy.

I promise, the ability to make decisions from a place of love and confidence is not only available to you; it is the key to living a purposeful and aligned life.

The hope I had for Steven is the same hope I have for you — that you will have the courage to leave behind what is no longer for you and step into the wild and fulfilling adventure that awaits.

In short, I hope you will get what you want and keep what you value.

DON'T GO ALONE

After our initial engagement, Steven joined a Forces at Work group I was leading. There were eight people in this group, and we met for six weeks. We discussed the material in this book as well as the questions you will find in the *Forces at Work Guidebook*.

Steven later told me this group was the catalyst for him to apply the principles he was learning, and it provided the accountability he needed to take the leap into his dream job. I encourage you to do the same. Who are six to eight personal or professional friends or acquaintances whom you would like to know better? Invite them to join you! Schedule six to eight times to meet as a group. Divide the chapters into reading assignments, and use the questions in the guidebook as the agenda for your meetings.

To learn more about groups that I am hosting, visit missyshopshire.com.

Reflection

Are there any parts of your day or week that you dread? How do you feel about the activities and projects that are on your calendar now? Do they light you up, or are you there by default or because of a commitment you made a long time ago? Do you recognize any places in your life where fear is holding you back? Where might fear be masquerading as responsibility in your life?

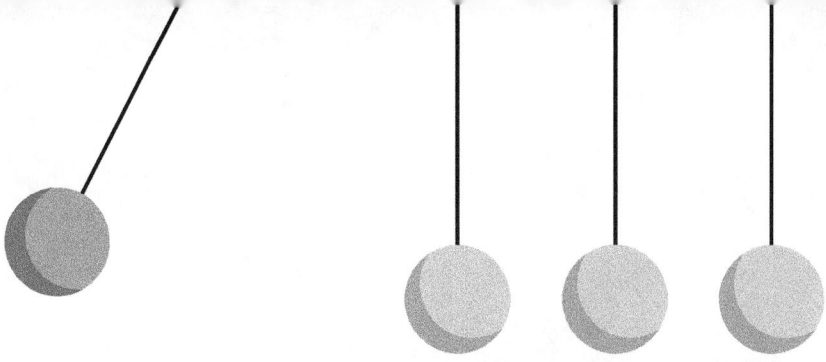

PART 2

begin with purpose

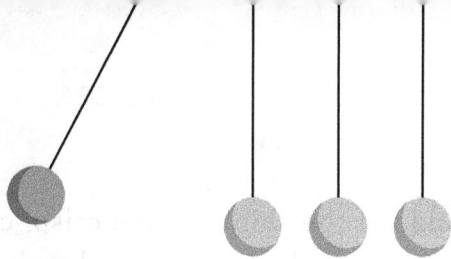

CHAPTER 3

spill the wind

"Love takes time, and hurry doesn't have it."

— John Mark Comer

I recently took a trip to the East Coast and spent four days on the *Mary Day*, a tall schooner harbored in Camden, Maine. The *Mary Day* is owned and captained by the Barry and Jen King family.

Being on this sailing ship is like going back in time. No engine powers the boat, and all the meals are cooked on a wood stove. The rustic, cramped cabins create more of a camping vibe than a luxury cruise experience. But what the *Mary Day* lacks in creature comforts, she makes up for in awe and wonder.

In the gentle chill of the morning, we woke to the smell of coffee and bacon, pulled on our sweatshirts, and climbed up to the deck to see a glorious sunrise. In the evenings, we wore light jackets and sipped bourbon as we sat under a million stars, their reflections mirrored in the water. In the mid-afternoon, when the sun warmed the deck, we dove off the side of the ship into the crisp, clear water. One afternoon, we dropped the anchor and took rowboats into a small cove, where we cooked lobsters, potatoes, and corn in large pots covered with seaweed.

For the *Mary Day*, wind is a commodity, and harnessing it requires the experience of a seasoned captain and a well-trained crew. When they succeed, get ready for a breathtaking ride. The magnificent sails fill, and the 100-foot boat cuts through the sea like an arrow through the forest.

I am a "more is better" person. During my second pregnancy, I had severe sciatica. It was always painful, but never more so than when I tried to lie down, making it exceedingly difficult to sleep. The first time I used Bengay to ease the pain, it allowed me to sleep for almost two hours in a row. I was impressed.

In fact, I figured if the recommended dose gave me so much relief, certainly applying three times the amount would allow me to sleep through the entire night! Within seconds, I regretted this decision, gasping in shock and jumping around like a monkey at the zoo. The burning on my traumatized backside took half an hour to subside. Lesson learned. More is not always better.

The same is true with the wind and the *Mary Day*. More wind creates more speed. But when the wind blows at a hard angle, the boat tilts in response. As exhilarating as it is to speed through the water, a high degree of tilt makes for a very uncomfortable journey — especially for the cook in the galley preparing meals for the 28 souls on board. An experienced captain knows when to spill the wind — to let enough wind out of the sails to right the boat.

Our lives are like this. We get so excited when we learn to harness the wind in our careers. We take off like a schooner on a clear day. As we develop our expertise and become capable of bigger achievements, our skill allows us to cover more ground faster. Then, our personal lives take off. We might add a few kids and some charitable work. We keep up with our friends from college and volunteer at school. Soon, our boat is tilting, but we just keep cooking on the woodstove — even though the dishes are sliding off the table and the kids are in danger of falling overboard. Our lives are in chaos, but killing the momentum is out of the question. It's just plain crazy talk, considering how hard we've worked to get it all moving in the right direction.

Clear the Decks

The next step toward alignment is to reconnect with your internal sense of purpose, but that is almost impossible if your boat is tilting from the sheer speed of your fast-paced life.

Why do we pack our schedules as tight as an overbooked flight on Sprint Airlines? What keeps us driving so hard and chasing more of everything? Lynne Twist tells us we have more opportunity and abundance in America than any other country in the world, but we also have the third highest incidence of anxiety and depression.[1] How can both things be true? Lynne argues that amidst all our abundance, most of us have a scarcity mentality.

What does this have to do with your tilting boat and your overbooked schedule? Lynne identifies three toxic myths that support a scarcity mindset. Let's see if any of them resonate with you.

Myth #1: "There isn't enough." There isn't enough pie for everyone, so I must rush in and grab what I can get before it's gone. This idea keeps us on high alert and always operating out of lack and desperation. We bookend our days with scarcity by telling ourselves in the morning, "I didn't get enough sleep," and at night, "I didn't get enough done." All the while, our souls cry out for rest, play, and meaning.

Myth #2: "More is better." What is more American than achieving your growth goal year after year? Lynne says, "It's the logical response if you fear there's not enough, but *more is better* drives a competitive culture of accumulation, acquisition, and greed that only heightens fears and quickens the pace of the race."[2] But we consider this to be progress. For most of us, doing less than we did last year is considered a failure or, at the very least, a setback.

Myth #3: "This is just the way things are." This belief is the fatal blow to any hope of restoring sanity to our lives. It breeds apathy and contributes to learned helplessness. When we choose to believe we can't do anything to change the situation, we give up our agency and go along with what everybody else is doing.

Welcome to the Present Moment

Before you book a cabin on the *Mary Day*, you need to know one thing: There is no destination. On our trip, we were at sea for four days and three nights, and we had no idea where we were going. This was intentional.

Our captain had been sailing these waters for 30 years, and he knew every cove and constellation like he knew the faces of his children. An itinerary would have cramped his style and diminished the adventure we enjoyed trusting his capable hands and his intuition as a sailor. As a result, we saw nature as it came to us — a sea of stars in an undiluted night sky, otters frolicking in the water, and the watchful eye of a majestic bald eagle examining our boats as we rowed toward its cove for our lobster feast.

Something magical happens when we surrender to the present moment. Early in my transformational journey, my coach told me, "Missy, who you are is more important than what you do." I loved and hated this statement. I'd spent a lifetime racking up accomplishments. My achievements made me feel like a winner, and on a deeper level, they made me feel like I was OK. But chasing them left me bone-weary and exhausted. The idea that I had value just for being who I was seemed fluffy and soft, but at the same time, it was a truth I longed to hear.

And if you are a recovering overachiever like me, you might need to be a force at rest before you can become a Force at Work.

I'm not suggesting you ditch your strategic plans and your personal goals forever. I am suggesting you let them go for a season and give yourself some room to breathe and to do some self-exploration. Who would you be without your goals or agenda? If this is a scary thought,

> If you are a recovering overachiever like me, you might need to be a force at rest before you can become a Force at Work.

begin by creating some unscheduled time in your calendar. Go for a walk. Read a book. See where it leads you. It might feel like a guilty pleasure, but I promise, it is necessary.

In stillness, we find clues leading to our next step. The power of your purpose is always in the present moment.

So, spill the wind. Release your destination for a season, and let's carve out a little time to wander.

A Word of Caution

In economics, there is a concept known as the J-Curve. It is a trend line that shows an initial loss immediately followed by a dramatic gain. Greg Overby, one of my favorite colleagues and a recovery coach, shared with me how this concept also applies to our personal growth.

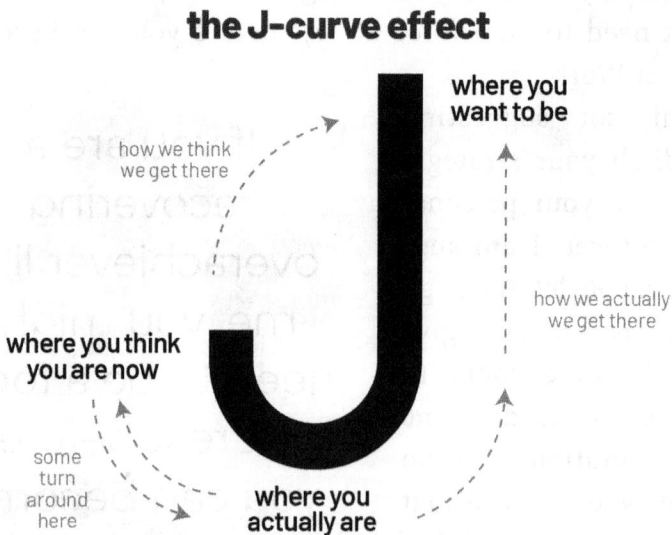

the J-curve effect

where you want to be

how we think we get there

how we actually we get there

where you think you are now

some turn around here

where you actually are

Sometimes creating space gives you time to look around and become overwhelmed by some disappointing aspects of your life. You might have been using denial to protect yourself from the full pain of your misalignment because you weren't ready to face it head-on. Melody Beatty says, "Denial can be confusing because it resembles sleeping. We're not really aware we are doing it until we're done doing it."[3]

When you remove the filter of denial, the hill you want to climb can suddenly loom larger.

But this is a normal part of the process. Stay the course. Like with the J-Curve, after an initial feeling of loss and overwhelm, you will experience dramatic progress as you restore sanity and integrity to your life and work. The journey will be worth it!

Explore Three Elements of Purpose

As you eliminate some activities and responsibilities in your life for a season, use this time to explore your purpose. The question we want to answer is, "What is your soul leading you to uncover now?"

Since purpose is a big idea and hard to wrangle, I find it helpful to approach it in three parts. And since one of my own strengths is getting to the point, I have a shortcut for each!

1. IDENTIFY YOUR CORE VALUES

In this first part, we'll identify your core values. These are the big ideas and universal themes that attract you at a deep level. Innate and unchanging, they are so fundamental to you that you might assume everyone else experiences them the same way. To a degree, they do, but you will express these values in your own unique way, and you also decide how to honor them. When we find ways to express our deepest core values, our authenticity blossoms.

Four pillars describe the most basic core values: Power, Love, Wisdom, and Knowledge. Each pillar also includes hundreds more subcategories. Lynn Taylor identifies these main pillars in his work through the Core Values Index Assessment™[4], which he created to help employers identify ideal candidates for specific roles within their companies. This is one of my favorite tools to help clients quickly identify and articulate their values.

> When we find ways to express our deepest core values, our authenticity blossoms.

I'll share a basic and brief overview of each value here.[5] You can find a link to the assessment on my website or by visiting taylorprotocols.com.

Power

If this is your primary value, you like to build things. You are at your best when you can invest your personal energy to create action and results. It's important for you to know what to do now and what to do next. You live in the now, and your learning style is "decide and do."

Love

This core value means you are primarily concerned with creating a positive vision of the future. You naturally nurture relationships and never tire of having meaningful conversations. It is important for you to know that others are being truthful with you and that all the cards are on the table. Your learning style is "talk and listen."

Wisdom

If this value is at your core, you probably love to solve problems. Your natural curiosity enables you to produce multiple options and innovative solutions for every problem. Empathy and compassion are important to you, and you have a unique ability to remain curious and empathetic regardless of the emotions and behavior of others. Your learning style is "assess and solve."

Knowledge

This value is often expressed through conservation of resources and by providing needed information. If this is your primary core value, you might geek out over research, facts, and data. You want information to be used justly and equitably, and you suspect many of the answers to our current problems can be found in the past, and you are energized by digging through the data to find them. Your learning style is "read and analyze."

These are high-level descriptions, and the assessment is essential to accurately determine yours — but hopefully, one or more of them has already resonated with you. My two primary core values are Power and Love. When I met Lynn Taylor for the first time, he said, "I bet you think your powerful love can solve anything." In one quick sentence, I felt as though he had seen my soul and read my mail!

2. REVISIT YOUR STRENGTHS

The second part of your purpose is your superpower or your strengths. These are the skills and aptitudes that come easily to you. Unlike core values, which are innate and largely unchanging, your strengths can be developed or declined. You have a propensity and natural skill for them, and you can train and improve them or neglect them and build others.

Decisions on developing or declining strengths are common sources of misalignment. Sometimes we have invested and built skills out of necessity, but they don't really resonate with us or bring us joy. Part of the work we want to do now is to revisit those strengths and see if you want to resurrect and develop any you previously declined. When my life felt like it was out of alignment, it was because I was overusing some of my strengths — sales, persuasion, teaching, and training. Instead, I wanted to lean into other skills — listening, coaching, inspiring, and speaking. I've found the easiest way to identify your strengths is by asking yourself the following questions:

1. What comes easily and naturally to me?
2. What do people come to me for?
3. What is my superpower, the one thing I seem to be better at than anyone else in the room?

Write out your answers to these questions. Notice any words that repeat. Pay attention to the strengths you most enjoy, and identify the ones you would rather bench.

3. CHOOSE YOUR MISSION

The final piece of your purpose is to define a mission. Your mission is a tangible expression of your values and strengths toward a specific outcome. Your mission identifies who you want to help and how you want to help them. By taking the key words from your core values work and your strengths, you can craft a mission statement. This written statement serves as an anchor as you make decisions about your future. You might have many different missions over the course of your life, but essentially one guiding purpose.

SAMPLE MISSION STATEMENT

This is an example of one of the early mission statements I crafted using my core values and strengths as I was just beginning my journey to express my truest purpose.

Values: Commitment, Truth, Positivity, Freedom

Strengths: Create, Connect, Impact, Compel

Mission: To free one thousand executives and entrepreneurs from their misalignment and golden handcuffs so they can achieve their potential and fully embrace their best lives.

Purpose Statement: I am committed to connecting with people and positively impacting their lives by compelling them with their own truth. (Connect and Compel)

---

elements of purpose

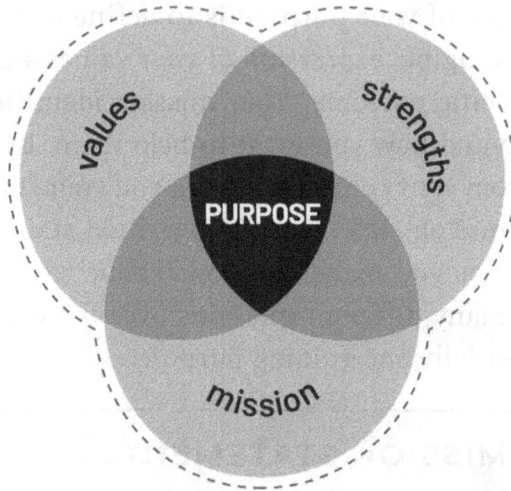

Doing this for the first time can be difficult and even frustrating, so don't aim for perfection. You are not marrying this purpose statement. Write the best one you can for now, set it aside, and keep reading. Trust the process. After you finish reading the entire book, go back and read your purpose statement with fresh eyes.

A great purpose statement crosses the boundary between your personal life and your professional life. Eventually, I whittled mine down to two words: Connect and Compel. These two words describe the essence of who I am, both at work and at home. I connect with others, listen to them, and persuade them to take the next step on their journeys. When I give myself permission to lean into these two words, I find the most joy and have the greatest impact on others.

Finding your purpose requires slowing down and reflecting for a season. Then, you can pick up the pieces of purpose —

your core values, strengths, and mission — and begin molding them into an expression of purpose that uniquely suits who you are now.

Reflection

How do you feel about the pace of your life right now? What would a slower, more intentional life look like for you? What words best describe your values? Your strengths? Your mission?

For more help writing out your mission and purpose statements, refer to your free *Forces at Work Guidebook*.

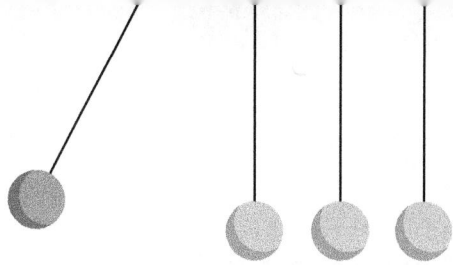

CHAPTER 4

dance
with desire

Desires are a compass for your life.

— David Neagle

When I met Melissa, she was the executive director of a non-profit organization that served sick children. She struck me as quiet, thoughtful, and servant hearted.

Our coaching arrangement was part of a larger leadership program for executive directors of nonprofit organizations. The program was an opportunity for these executive directors to grow their leadership skills and surround themselves with other leaders who understood the unique challenges of working with a board, dealing with donors, and serving populations that were hurting.

I could see right away Melissa was a capable leader, but I sensed her misalignment. Good-hearted weariness often masks misalignment, and Melissa seemed weary. She presented a picture of dedication and faithful service, but I noticed that during our conversations, she used the word "should" a lot. "Should" is another clue to misalignment. But the biggest clue? Although Melissa was a diligent worker and dedicated to the organization, I couldn't see an ounce of joy as she described her work. In fact, joy was noticeably missing.

Since Melissa came to the coaching relationship through her organization, she expected the focus of our conversations to be on her role as an executive director. I assured her that my priority was to coach her as a person first, and then as the leader of the organization. I wanted to give her the freedom to explore whatever was standing in front of her joy.

Look for the Sparks

During one of our early conversations, we somehow got on the subject of living in France. My husband and I celebrated our anniversary there, and this had come up in our discussion. Melissa made a passing comment: "We've talked about spending a year in France with our kids."

A year? This surprised me. It seemed so out of place from the life she had described to me, living in rural Indiana, raising three kids, and knee-deep in the demands of a local charity. But this was the first spark of joy I had seen in her since we started working together.

I have learned to trust and follow the little sparks of joy I see in my clients. Like a small splash of color landing on a gray canvas, it evoked my curiosity, and I wanted to learn more.

It seemed completely out of place in light of the issues we were tackling for the organization, but I sensed she was burying the lead on the third page of the paper.

A simple step in finding your purpose is to pause and pay attention to times when you feel joy and a spark of creativity.

I gently drew her back to this topic. As we explored this desire, she shared that her husband grew up in the French countryside, and they had always dreamed of giving their kids, ages ten, nine, and seven, at least one year in France to experience the culture.

> A simple step in finding your purpose is to pause and pay attention to times when you feel joy and a spark of creativity.

She explained more about how she and her husband had first met and how she had been involved in international work before moving to Indiana. As she shared, she became more excited, and her countenance changed completely. Now we were getting somewhere! I quickly realized this wasn't a passing fantasy; it was deeply rooted in her values and her desires. It had all the earmarks of purpose.

The Desires of Your Heart

Melissa's faith is important to her. She loves God and wants to live a life that honors Him. I saw that her desire had gotten twisted up in a picture of service that valued sacrifice and martyrdom over adventure and creativity. She had stopped dreaming about what she wanted because those dreams felt selfish and frivolous. With only good intentions, she had traded her dreams for a life of service that had morphed into sacrifice. Sometimes making sacrifices is noble, but when our need to sacrifice hijacks our desire to serve, we create a life marked by misery and compulsion. Resentment is not far behind.

Faith and service are important to me, too. I could relate to Melissa's struggle.

In recent years, my belief about desire has shifted. I used to think listening to my desires was selfish, or at the very least, it came last. Indulging in a desire was a reward reserved for after I finished everything I was "supposed to do." My desires got the leftovers, and for all intents and purposes, God was separate from them.

> When our need to sacrifice hijacks our desire to serve, we create a life marked by misery and compulsion.

And then, one day, I found a verse in the Bible: "Delight yourself in the Lord, and He will give you the desires of your heart" (Psalm 37:4, ESV). I had heard it hundreds of times, but this time it hit differently. You can read it in two ways. Here's the first: Like a benevolent father, God gives us what we want. The second way differs: As a loving and wise co-creator, God gives us *what to want*.

I like the second version better. I believe that God, Love, the Universe, whoever you see as your higher power, is our co-creator and gives us clues to our role and our growth through our desires. Our desires are not selfish;

they are significant. We can learn a lot by paying attention to them and following what ignites our joy. Simply put, when we pursue our desires, we step into our purpose.

> When we pursue our desires, we step into our purpose.

Clues from the Past

Looking back, I can see clues to my own purpose from things that brought joy to me as a child.

On my fourth birthday, my parents gave me a toy phone. It was pink, and I loved that it had push buttons instead of a rotary dial, which was more common at the time. (Yes, I am that old.) The little buttons dinged delightfully when I pushed them. My imagination instantly transported me to a fantasy office where I had important projects and decisions to make. I spent hours making and taking imaginary calls with abandon. This magical phone transformed me into a business fairy princess. I'm not sure where I got my idea of what business was — my dad was in the navy and my mom was a full-time homemaker — but the idea of meetings, decisions, and giving direction drew me in at an early age.

The intrigue with the play phone was a clue to my purpose.

As a coach, I spend the better part of my day on the phone. I have replaced the pink toy with an iPhone and some AirPods, but this is where I am most comfortable in my work. I often walk around a nearby lake in my neighborhood or through a wooded park while I am coaching my clients on the phone.

When I was feeling misaligned and trapped in my sales career, my coach encouraged me to write down all the things I loved about my current role and what I no longer wanted to do. It was so hard for me to let go of what made sense and what I still felt I "had to" do or "should" do. She kept challenging me to strip the list back by asking, "If you didn't *have to* do anything, what would you *want* to do?"

The part I loved was coaching people and helping them reach their goals. It sounds crazy, but during our conversations, I could see potential and possibilities in them that they couldn't yet see in themselves. The part I no longer wanted to do was selling cosmetics, managing inventory, handling administrative details, and doing the training that had become so tiring to me.

"I want to be a professional friend," I finally blurted out.

I cringed when I heard the words out loud. A professional friend? That sounds so cheesy and dumb, I thought.

My coach did not laugh or discount the idea. She encouraged me to keep talking about it. Through these conversations, I began to believe I could be a professional coach who felt like a friend. I still had doubts and wondered if anyone would pay me for this. I took courses to become a coach, learning how to remain objective and to offer tools and frameworks to help people move through challenges and find their own answers.

It was challenging work, but it sparked my joy and my natural curiosity. I loved learning how to have effective coaching conversations. I nerded out over concepts like neuro resonance and neuro dissonance. I felt like I had been given the keys to the city when I learned how to position myself as an ally instead of an adversary when sharing feedback with my clients.

The clarity of showing up as a professional friend helped me stand strong when a marketing company told me I had to decide whether I was a personal life coach or a business coach. I saw myself as both — a life coach in a business environment. I put "Business Life Coach" on my business cards, and it felt right. I enjoy supporting clients in both their personal and professional endeavors. The other day, a client told me I was the Swiss army knife of coaching. That comment made my day!

I also enjoy dear friendships with my former clients. These relationships are important to me. Following my desire has added so much richness and fullness to my life.

I wanted to help Melissa follow her desires, too. Melissa signed on to the executive director job because it seemed to fit with her value to serve. When we dug a little deeper, she shared that even when she first took the job, her head was in it, but her heart was not fully engaged. Without another clear alternative, she had made what seemed like the most logical decision at the time.

If It's Not Good for You, It's Not Good for Them

Now that Melissa was seeing the truth of the situation, she realized this role wasn't a good fit for her. But even with this revelation, she wasn't quite ready to leave.

Melissa felt indispensable to the organization and could not imagine leaving them in the lurch. Loyal to the core, this is one reason many of my clients struggle to leave their current roles. They have taken on the weight of the world and feel like they are holding everything together. For Melissa, I gently suggested that if this situation was not good for her, it wasn't good for her organization, either. Her leaving would give the organization an opportunity to put someone in this role who found greater joy and fulfillment in it.

Any time I am hired to coach for a company, I know one of the potential outcomes is that my client might leave the company that is paying for their coaching. I no longer let this bother me because, either way, it is still a win for the company. Getting to the truth and celebrating when people move on to their next role is a hallmark of a healthy culture.

The more Melissa and I talked about Project France, the more excited she became. A million obstacles — real and imagined — still stood in the way, but as Melissa and I continued to focus on who she wanted to be instead of how she wanted others to perceive her, she came alive.

Unexpected Detours

Halfway through our coaching agreement, the pandemic started. This disrupted the entire world and presented enormous challenges for organizations like Melissa's. True to the J-Curve, once Melissa had a taste of what was possible, it was harder to run from the truth that her day-to-day work was draining her. And now we had a pandemic and all its challenges to deal with. Melissa put her energy and time into the organization but *made a decision* to move her family to France. She and her husband began working out the details, and Melissa and I began to create a new vision for her career.

Then, something extraordinary happened.

Melissa and her husband had volunteered as members of a global economic forum, an organization made up of committed people coming together to solve some of the world's biggest challenges. The couple attended an annual conference and kept up on a variety of issues in many countries all over the world.

In August of 2021, the US left Afghanistan, creating a cascading string of events beginning with a quick and chaotic evacuation of military forces. The Taliban quickly took control. Thousands upon thousands of Afghan men, women, and children, particularly people of specific minorities or those who had helped in democratic movements and women's rights, were desperate to leave due to the Taliban's threats against their lives.

The economic forum members quickly met and jumped into action to help evacuate as many vulnerable people as possible. They created a separate elite team to work under the umbrella of the larger organization. During one meeting, Melissa mentioned she used to work in relocation, and she also had contacts in international immigration that might be helpful. So, she and her husband put together a small cohort to give strategic support for the people still on the ground in Afghanistan. For the next several months, they worked around the clock in addition to their regular jobs, rescuing vulnerable people from the terror of the Taliban.

Their efforts saved thousands of lives. Stepping into this opportunity energized Melissa and made her feel alive. During our previous sessions, I had Melissa create a description of her dream job. It was uncanny how this opportunity appeared and matched her description. Even though it was a volunteer opportunity, it was so much more rewarding than her current paid role, and she was finally ready to resign. Within days, she received inquiries from a few of the connections she had met through the Afghanistan project, asking about future opportunities and ways she could contribute similarly on a bigger stage.

As I write, she is taking it all in and considering these opportunities. And she is doing it from France. A few months ago, she and her husband moved their family and are now living out their dream. Using their new home as a launch pad, they have already taken the kids to visit London, Dubai, and South Africa. Had she not been willing to go through the coaching process and face the pain of her misalignment, she might never have left her original job.

Melissa is a Force at Work. She is more confidently leaning into her desires to inform her purpose, trusting that the process will continue to lead her to opportunities and projects that bring meaning and ignite her passion.

Reflection

On a scale of 1–10, how much joy does your life and work bring you right now? Feel free to rate them separately.

If your number-one goal was to experience more joy in your life, how could you move that number closer to a 10?

Do you remember any clues from your childhood that spark joy in you? What did you love to do as a child?

Where might you be staying stuck in agreements because you don't want to let someone down? How could you end or amend those commitments with grace?

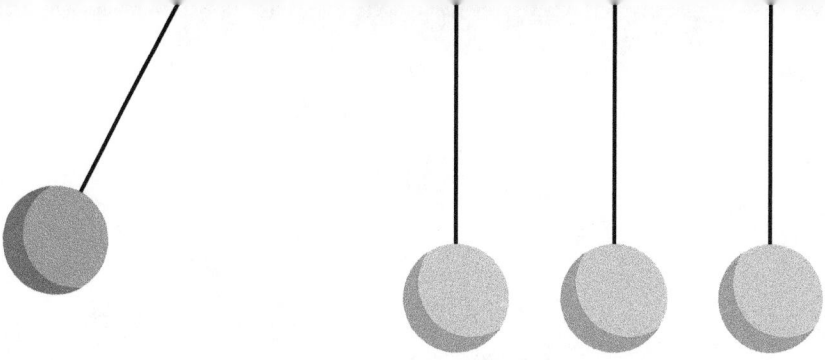

create a compelling vision

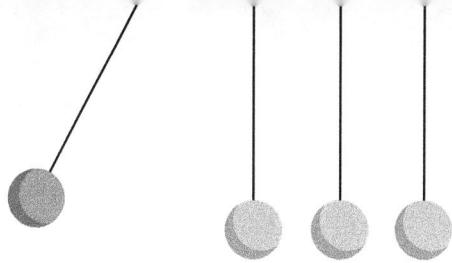

CHAPTER 5

let your dream lead

People don't change because of what they know to be true, but rather because of what they believe to be possible.

— Neil Gordon

A few years ago, my husband was having coffee in Indianapolis with a few of his colleagues. Ironically, Adam doesn't like coffee. If he's out with a group, he'll order one and then proceed to obliterate any coffee taste by adding copious amounts of cream and sugar. On this day, the only cream available was in those tiny containers where you peel off the paper lid and pour it in one thimbleful at a time. As Adam tediously prepared his Kool-Aid coffee, he joked with the guys, "I bet they use these little creamers on the space station."

A woman near him laughed. She turned around, still smiling, and said, "That's not at all what we use in space."

Adam learned her name is Anousheh Ansari, and she had come to Indianapolis to speak about a little trip she took to the International Space Station. Later that evening, when he told me about his encounter with her, my jaw dropped. Curiosity sparked, and I went straight to Mother Google to learn everything I could about this fascinating woman who seemed to know all the ins and outs of drinking coffee in space.

I discovered that Anousheh was born in Iran on September 12, 1966. I knew enough about Iran to recognize it was not the most fertile soil for aspiring women. Girls there face tremendous obstacles on their way to basic human rights, including education. How did she become an astronaut?

Anousheh's Story

As a little girl, Anousheh loved the stars, and she had a habit of going outside to look at the night sky. It filled her with a deep curiosity and wonder, and gazing at the stars gave her a sense of peace. As she looked up at the constellations, her imagination would sweep her away, and she would dream of traveling among the stars.

But children have fantasies like this all the time. You could ask a room full of kids what they want to be when they grow up, and a handful of them will tell you, "I'm going to be an astronaut!" We smile and nod in encouragement though we know it is statistically quite unlikely — and how much more so for a little girl living in a war-torn country where women are marginalized and oppressed?

But space travel remained a recurring dream and an unrelenting curiosity for Anousheh. When she was five, she drew a picture of a spaceship and showed it to everyone in her family, emphatically telling them she would be going to space.

When she was twelve, the Iranian Revolution happened, followed by war. Gunshots, burning buildings, bombings, alarms, blackouts, and food rationing violently disrupted Anousheh's daily life. Again, she found refuge in the night sky, stealing away to her backyard, where her imagination took her away into her dream of going to space. The stars became her passion.

Whenever possible, she fed her curiosity by reading science fiction and by watching Star Trek.

As a teenager, Anousheh came to the United States, where she attended college to study engineering. Her one disappointment in coming to the States was learning that Starfleet Academy was, in fact, a fictional place made up by Hollywood. Anousheh graduated with an engineering degree and began a career in telecommunications. She continued to work hard. Remarkably, she never stopped nurturing her curiosity about space travel. And eventually, her curiosity led to an extraordinary outcome.

On September 18, 2006, Anousheh lifted off into space, arriving at the International Space Station two days later. (You can read more about this incredible journey and her other accomplishments in her captivating autobiography.[6])

I tell this story often and am always shocked that almost no one in my audience has ever heard of Anousheh Ansari. It baffles me, honestly. This little girl from Iran dreamed about being an astronaut AND. MADE. IT. TO. THE. SPACE. STATION.

What I love most about her story is how she nurtured her childhood dream.

If you watch Anousheh's TED Talk, you will see a picture of the rocket she drew at age five.[7] Next to this image, she shares a photo of the actual rocket that took her to space. (If it does not give you chills, please check your pulse and seek medical attention immediately.)

Anousheh did not take the conventional path to space because it was unavailable to her. Remarkably, in a world of skeptics and harsh realities, she nurtured her imagination and kept her curiosity alive, choosing to save room for another possibility. In doing so, she allowed her conscious and unconscious mind to pay attention to resources and opportunities that she might otherwise have dismissed. This allowed her imagination to inform the decisions she made and the opportunities she pursued, creating a new path.

Perhaps this is why Albert Einstein so famously said, "Imagination is more important than knowledge."

Anousheh Ansari is a Force at Work.

Her story reminds us how truly little in our world has been accomplished or invented without first being imagined.

Memory or Imagination

In any circumstance, we each have a vision or a picture in our heads of how we think things are going to turn out. Our non-conscious brains work day and night to help us bring this vision into reality. This is the same powerful part of the brain that takes care of all the other things we do on autopilot, like breathing, temperature regulation, and cell division.

The Reticular Activating System (RAS), also part of the non-conscious brain, determines what we pay attention to.

Once, I went with my husband to test-drive new cars. Having graciously driven the Pink Cadillacs I earned in my sales career for many years, he was ready for something a little more manly that he could proudly drive to Lowes on a Saturday. While there, we drove a red Jeep. In the end, he didn't buy it, but I still see red Jeeps every day. I have essentially programmed my brain to look for red Jeeps.

Your vision is simply a mental picture of success and the program you input for your brain to follow. You have two resources from which to choose when creating this vision: It can come from memory or from imagination.

For most of us, memory becomes our default source as we age. We collect memories because they help us make sense of the world. They teach us not to touch a hot stove. They remind us of what has and has not worked for us in the past.

But, when we rely too heavily on memory to feed our vision, we are left to recreate similar versions of things we have already done. By using only what we know to be true from the past, we can easily get stuck in a rut.

In contrast, little children naturally rely on imagination because they don't have catalogs full of memories. If we can access our child-like imaginations as adults, as Anousheh did, we can open limitless possibilities for our future.

So how do we engage our imagination to ignite our vision?

Stay Curious

Albert Einstein, among all his other achievements, was first a champion of the adult imagination. Though arguably one of the most gifted people who ever lived, he is famous for saying, "I have no special talent. I am only passionately curious."

As a business coach, I have seen the power of curiosity win the day. Judgment, sarcasm, and criticism have invaded our personal and professional relationships like pervasive weeds. If you can remain empathetic and curious regardless of current events, disappointments, and the behavior of others, you possess an incredible and rare superpower.

The opposite of curiosity is judgment. From the moment we wake up each day, we make judgments about everything — the weather, our breakfast, our appearance, our colleagues.

Judgment puts us in an "either/or" frame of mind. This approach is the fastest way to shut off creative solutions and kill imagination. In the face of judgment, fear pulls us toward what is familiar or what feels tried and true.

There is an old story about a little girl who was in the kitchen with her mother on Christmas Eve. They were getting ready to put the ham in the oven, and the mother took a knife and cut off the ends of the ham.

"Mommy," the little girl asked, "why do you cut off the ends of the ham?"

The mother paused. "Honestly, I'm not sure," she said. "But this is how my mother taught me."

The little girl ran to the living room, where her grandma was sitting.

"Grandma, why do you cut off the ends of the ham?" the little girl asked.

Her grandma replied, "My mother taught me to do it that way." She looked over to the chair where the little girl's great-grandmother was sitting.

The little girl asked one more time, "Great-Grandma, why do we cut off the ends of the ham?"

The great-grandma smiled, looking at the other women before she replied, "I'm not sure why *they* do it, but *I* did it because my pan was too small."

Just like this little girl did, we can use our curiosity to challenge the status quo.

Find Meaning

Anousheh faced many challenges personally and professionally. How did she stay positive after experiencing the ravages of war, the divorce of her parents, and the challenges of being an immigrant in a land so different from the one she had known?

The larger question is, how do we manage our emotional responses when we face circumstances that seem insurmountable? Circumstances such as a broken marriage, a sick child, a chronic illness, or a financial burden can weigh us down. How do some people hold room for reaching their potential while others allow these difficult circumstances to defeat them?

Ever since reading *Man's Search for Meaning*[8] in high school, I have sought to emulate the life and example of Viktor Frankl. He believed meaning is a central motivational force and a factor in mental health. We can thank him for providing the foundational principles for the field of positive psychology — principles that are transforming lives and helping people reach their potential today.[9]

His life circumstances were remarkable. Though he spent four years in concentration camps and lost both parents, his wife, and his brother to Hitler's evil regime, his undaunted perspective is a concrete example that we can find meaning even in the direst and most hopeless of circumstances.

Viktor wrote, "Between stimulus and response, there is a space. In that space is our power to choose our response. In our response lies our growth and our freedom."

We do not always get to choose the stimulus, but we do get to choose our response. Anousheh did not choose the revolution or the war. She chose how she responded to it by chasing meaningful pursuits and keeping her vision alive. Viktor did not choose to be held captive in a slave camp or to have his family brutally murdered, but he chose dignity in the face of these things. Both Anousheh and Victor were Forces at Work who went on to make valuable contributions to the world despite the things that happened to them.

> We do not always get to choose the stimulus, but we do get to choose our response.

In his book *Success Principles*, Jack Canfield also writes about the power of our response in difficult circumstances. He shares an effective, easy-to-remember formula for success:

E+R=O, or "Event plus Response equals Outcome."[10]

The most recent example of a collective opportunity to choose our response in difficult circumstances is the global pandemic. It impacted each of us to varying degrees.

First, I want to acknowledge that my role in the pandemic differed vastly from those of my friends who were healthcare workers and public safety officials. At ground zero, this event had many more drastic implications for their lives and called many of them into extraordinary and often heartbreaking service. And yet, like Viktor Frankl, they also retained the one human dignity that can never be taken away — the power to choose their response. During difficult times, our collective vision can grow dim. Perhaps the greatest gift we can give others is to hold out hope and do whatever is in our power to alleviate the suffering we see.

Though I was not in the pandemic's epicenter, my first response was fear. I went into survival mode, securing masks for my family and stocking up on zinc lozenges, vitamin C, and toilet paper. I stayed awake at night worrying about each member of my family, vigilantly watching updates on the news and imagining exactly what I would do if one of us got sick.

> During difficult times, our collective vision can grow dim.

But as the months wore on, I began to choose peace. Every morning, I reminded myself I could choose my response to what was happening. I took reasonable precautions, but I turned the TV off. I enjoyed the slowness of life and the joy of having my family together as we worked and studied from home.

Some of our most treasured family moments occurred amid this global turmoil. We held a small wedding for my daughter in our backyard, a simple affair full of beauty, love, and hope. A few days later, I celebrated my fiftieth birthday, and my family gave me a thirty-day sabbatical to Ft. Myers Beach by myself. This was an incredible gift, and I know I was privileged to be able to go.

During the thirty days of my sabbatical, I walked on the beach, read books, and wrote in my journal. As the pandemic raged on, I became grounded again. The time I spent alone reminded me I could contribute to the chaos by letting fear reign, or I could choose a response grounded in love and faith.

If Viktor Frankl had lived through the pandemic with us, I think he would have reminded us not to underestimate the power of our response to affect the outcome in any situation, no matter how dire it seems. He would have affirmed that no matter whether we find ourselves on the frontline or on the sideline during an experience, we retain our right to choose our response.

Your imagination answers to your mind, and it will go down whatever road you ask it to. Why not direct it toward the most positive outcome you can imagine? Instead of asking it to keep showing you the worst thing that can happen, how about asking it to show you the best?

Even in difficult circumstances, we have the power to respond in love and hope instead of giving in to fear and despair.

Reflection

What was your biggest fantasy as a child? What about it still appeals to you today? What difficult circumstances are you facing? What response will you choose?

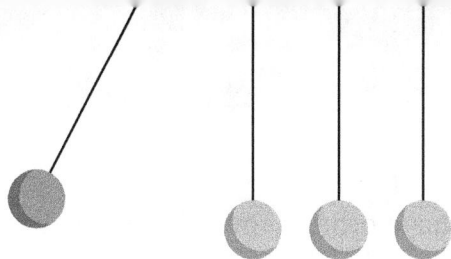

CHAPTER 6

ditch the dragon; date the dreamer

"A vision is not just a picture of what could be;
it is an appeal to our better selves,
a call to become something more."

— Rosabeth Moss Kanter

W e all have an internal dialogue going on in our heads, and often it sounds like an argument between two voices. I call these voices the Dreamer and the Dragon.

The Dreamer is the voice of love and possibility, also known as our visionary. It wants us to reach our full potential and to step into our highest aspirations for our lives and our careers.

The Dragon is the voice of fear and the status quo. It wants to keep us safe and avoid change of any kind. We have other names for this voice. Some of us know it as the ego, the skeptic, or the critic. My client Brooke named her Dragon "Alice."

These two voices hold vastly different priorities, and they are often in conflict. The Dragon fights to protect the personality and worries about how others will perceive us. On the other hand, the Dreamer wants to honor the soul, helping us find our purpose and make a valuable contribution to the world. The Dreamer calls us to be brave and take risks, but the Dragon is hell-bent on keeping us safe inside the hollow mountain.

Others, namely our parents, friends, teachers, and siblings, have influenced these voices throughout our lives. These formative influencers may have nurtured your Dreamer and told you that you could do anything you set your mind to. They may have helped you frame your failures as minor setbacks. Or, you might have had a more skeptical voice constantly summoning the Dragon by whispering doubt and criticism over you.

Do you remember the pink phone my parents gave me on my fourth birthday — the one that turned me into a magical business fairy princess and pointed me toward my career as a coach? There is more to that story.

The morning *after* my fourth birthday, I woke up early, snuck into the kitchen, and started making calls. I am not sure how long I was there, but soon, a shadow appeared, ripped the phone from my little hands, opened the door to the basement, and sent my precious phone crashing down the stairs. Then the shadow, who turned out to be my dad, slammed the door and gruffly ordered me back to my room.

Trembling, I crawled back into my bed. This was the first time I remember experiencing terror at the hands of my father, and it wouldn't be the last. Because I didn't have the tools to process his erratic behavior, my Dragon stepped in to protect me. I became hypervigilant and learned to read my dad's moods. I could sense when he was about to come unglued, and my Dragon warned me when to avoid him or hide. I carried this childhood survival response with me into adulthood.

My dad often criticized my behavior in destructive ways.

When I was seven or eight, he put two pieces of cake in front of me and asked me to choose the one I wanted.

"Go ahead and take the one you really want," he coaxed.

I hated these games. I knew he was trying to teach me a lesson, and at this young age, I already knew there was no right answer. I picked the larger piece.

"I knew you would pick this one," he said, pushing it toward me. "I think you are a selfish little girl," he concluded, shaking his head.

He may have said more, but I didn't hear it. My throat swelled shut, and tears sprang to my eyes. Shame overwhelmed me, so I couldn't even take a bite. But the Dragon inside me swallowed every bit of the message — I was a selfish nuisance and a disappointment.

I decided I never wanted to feel that bad again, so, at any hint of selfishness, I allowed my Dragon to scream at me like an angry drill sergeant. As a result, I overcompensated, bending over backward for others and deferring to everyone around me. For years, I struggled with healthy self-care because it felt selfish and indulgent.

WHICH VOICE DO YOU HEAR?

Dreamer's Voice	Dragon's Voice
• inspires you	• confuses you
• calms you	• pushes you
• reassures you	• discourages you
• enlightens you	• criticizes you
• encourages you	• worries you
• invites you	• threatens you

When our internal Dragon gets drunk on power, he takes over. He tries to anticipate every pitfall and danger we might encounter. He bombards us with warnings of our weakness and shoots ammunition he has collected from our failures. As we try to stave off each assault, staying safe trumps stepping out. It is exhausting. And dreams? Who has the energy for anything as frivolous as a dream?

Conviction Vs. Condemnation

One way we ditch the Dragon's shame tactics is by distinguishing between conviction and condemnation.

The Dragon has valuable information we need to hear. My pretend phone calls first thing in the morning probably annoyed my parents. And, of course, it is impolite to take the biggest piece of cake. But in a spirit of condemnation, this information can paralyze the receiver with shame. Condemnation is a foreboding rain cloud that covers the sky when you're outdoors; it leaves you feeling exposed and unprepared for life. It suggests you are "bad," and it does not distinguish you from your behavior. It leads to fear and despair and offers no remedy for correction.

Conviction, on the other hand, is extremely specific. Although it can also be painful, it comes from a place of love and confidence. Conviction is the voice of the Dreamer, urging you to learn a lesson and restore integrity with your own values. As adults, if we take a brave minute to listen to the voice of conviction, it will give us a specific action or step we can take to restore alignment within ourselves.

While building my direct sale business, I often felt guilty. When I was working, I felt guilty for not being with the kids. But when I was with the kids, I felt guilty for not working. Almost every working mom I know has engaged in this type of guilt cycle at some point or another.

The Dragon in my head accused me, "You are a bad mom. You are neglecting your kids *and* shirking your responsibilities at work."

This general judgment reflected my worst fear. Condemnation knocks you down and then hands you a problem too big to solve.

> Condemnation knocks you down and then hands you a problem too big to solve.

IMAGINATION SETS YOU FREE

Surprisingly, one of the most powerful and overlooked tools to overcome the voice of condemnation is your own imagination.

And the simplest and easiest way to access your imagination is by asking questions. My internal process goes something like this.

The thought presents itself: "You are a bad mom."

First, I observe the thought. I choose to pause and stay curious. I resist the urge to take the bait and go looking for evidence to support this negative thought. I take a deep breath.

Then, I ask a question. "Well, what would a good mom do?" Since this is my goal, it makes sense to start there. Instead of automatically looking for evidence I am a bad mom, I redirect my brain toward a solution.

I take a minute to reflect. What would a good mom do right now? I conjure up a mental picture of what a good mom looks like, and then I let my imagination take the lead. Maybe a good mom would stop working when her kids got home from school and would emotionally connect with them and ask about their day. Maybe she would just check in with them and ask if they needed anything. I visualize this happening and write down anything that seems actionable.

Then, I choose one action I can take immediately. What would a good mom do right now? Remember, our power is not in the past nor in the future; it is always and only in the very present moment.

> Our power is not in the past nor in the future; it is always and only in the very present moment.

When my daughter, Grace, was 14 years old, I was feeling particularly stretched between my business and my family. Grace loved to watch *The Gilmore Girls* when she got home from school. Even though I generally loathe TV and watching during the day feels like an affront to my productivity, I decided to sit down and watch at least one episode with her every day after school. Watching TV as an act of model motherhood was counterintuitive and didn't come easily for me, but I used this time to reconnect with her. Soon, I found myself anxious for her to get off the bus so I could end my workday early, and we could crash together on the couch.

At the end of each year, I ask the kids to write out their highlights. That year, Grace did not list the pricey VIP tickets I bought for the meet and greet with the *Dancing with the Stars* cast, nor did she mention our trip to Disneyland. She said, "Mom, I think we grew so much closer this year by watching *The Gilmore Girls* together."

Eradicating guilt doesn't always require an extravagant solution. A small, inspired action can quiet the Dragon and restore your vision in quick time.

> A small, inspired action can quiet the Dragon and restore your vision in quick time.

Make the Dragon Your Ally

Though the Dreamer and the Dragon are conflicting voices with different priorities, they both have valuable information to share, and they are both looking for the same thing: evidence. The Dragon doesn't have to be your enemy. The key to making him your ally is to know what he wants. Here are some ways to win him over.

1. FIND EVIDENCE FOR YOUR SUCCESS

Each of us has an internal filing cabinet where we keep evidence for our success and failure. For some reason, we effortlessly remember our failures, but it takes awareness and intention not to dismiss our successes. The loudest voice in our head is often the Dragon. He points out failure so we don't get too far ahead of ourselves. The Dreamer draws us to possibilities. But those get lost in the noise when the Dragon is roaring with fire and chasing us back into the hollow mountain. Finding evidence for your success is also referred to as learned optimism. This essentially means you are just as committed to noticing your wins as you are to noticing your perceived failures.

2. WRITE DOWN YOUR PURPOSE AND VISION

Since both the Dreamer and the Dragon are looking for evidence, alignment is critical. In the absence of a guiding purpose and a compelling vision, the Dragon relentlessly defends the status quo. Without these key pieces in place, there is no reason to risk change by letting you out of the cave of mediocrity. However, if you write out your purpose statement and your vision, the Dragon, though cautious, will become more of an ally who points out areas of concern or potential pitfalls.

3. HAVE A STRATEGY

Once the Dragon knows you have a purpose and a vision in place, he just wants to know you have a strategy to address the real or imagined obstacles you may face. You can create a strategy by writing down each fear. Then, line by line, answer, "What would I do if this actually happened?"

4. PRESERVE YOUR INTEGRITY

You need one more crucial element before the Dragon will surrender as an adversary and become an ally: ruthless integrity with yourself.

Since the Dragon keeps us safe by pointing out inconsistencies and potential pitfalls, it is critical that you keep the agreements you make with yourself and with others. When you don't do what you say you are going to do, the Dragon takes note. So don't make excuses or bury a broken agreement under the rug. Deal with it honestly. If you are late, apologize and change your behavior so you can be on time. In my experience, it is always better to under-promise and over-deliver because small inconsistencies add up. Although we will never be perfect, we can bridge the gap between what we promise to do and what we actually deliver.

Get Your Dreamer and Dragon to Work Together

The Dragon will prematurely demand answers and push you to create strategies before you have fully developed your vision. Strategy forces you to be realistic, and if this happens too early, your dreams are compromised, and the vision will suffer. Here are five suggestions to co-opt a healthy partnership between these two entities.

1. ESCORT THE DRAGON TO THE WAITING ROOM

Ironically, the first step in getting the Dreamer and the Dragon to work together is to split them up. The Dreamer's vision is powerful, but before it is fully expressed, it is vulnerable to being squashed by the Dragon's desire for strategy. Since the Dragon just cannot help but interrupt the visioning process, he can't be allowed near it.

Coaches are trained to help you with this. During the vision section of my Forces at Work coaching program, I have been known to physically walk my clients out of my office and ask them to leave the skeptic in a chair in the waiting room before we return to talk about their vision.

2. GIVE EVEN MORE TIME TO YOUR DREAMER

I hope you are beginning to see that the Dreamer and the Dragon both have roles to play in your success. The Dragon is used to hogging the airtime, so you must intentionally carve out space to use your imagination and dream.

> You must carve out space to use your imagination and dream.

3. GIVE YOUR DREAMER SPACE TO ROAM

When working with your Dreamer, do not tie her to reality. She must be able to give you a grand vision unclouded by practicality or any obstacles you are currently facing.

4. INVITE THE DRAGON'S FEEDBACK

After you have a clear and compelling vision for what you want to create with any project or endeavor, invite the Dragon back into the conversation. The Dragon will share his concerns and note any inconsistencies, which you can write down and address systematically.

When you have a dream, only two things will keep you from reaching it: a limiting belief or an external obstacle. The dragon will happily fill you in on each of them and warn you of any challenges ahead. Limiting beliefs will require new, more empowering beliefs, and the obstacles will require specific strategies.

5. WORK WITH A COACH

Even when you mentally separate the Dreamer and the Dragon, the Dragon can still get out of hand. Doing this work with someone you know who has a stake in the outcome always risks their Dragon jumping in, too. Instead, consider working with an objective coach who knows how to wrangle the Dragon and empower the Dreamer.

Skeptics will demand you have all the answers and resources before you act on your dream. But coaches know that dreams don't work that way. You can only see as far as you can see, and you cannot solve tomorrow's problems with today's resources. As you take each step, you will face challenges, but new resources and connections will also become available. A coach can help you uncover these resources and provide the perspective and encouragement you need to keep going.

COACHING OR THERAPY: WHICH IS THE RIGHT FIT?

I have spent time in therapy over the years to heal the broken messages I received as a child and to tame the Dragon in my head. This is an appropriate time to talk about the difference between coaching and therapy.

Generally speaking, coaching is about moving forward, and therapy is about healing hurt from the past.

Greg Overby, my colleague who taught me about the J-Curve, was an affiliate coach with my company for a few years. Before becoming a coach, he was a licensed therapist. He taught me to look for things that would indicate a need to refer a client for therapy in addition to or instead of coaching.

He said if a client cannot consistently follow through on their commitments or points of accountability in the coaching space, something deeper may be going on. They may need to work with a therapist to help them explore further.

He suggested the rule of three: The first time a client misses a commitment, we look at what happened and adjust our strategy. The second time, we do the same. By the third time, if the client is still stuck on the same issue, thought pattern, or behavior, it's time to call in reinforcements.

I always have this conversation with my clients after the second miss. If this resonates with you, you'll want to find a trained therapist to help you heal. You can put your coaching on hold, or you can continue with both resources working together. Many of my clients successfully engage in therapy and coaching at the same time.

Extra: Don't Feed the Other Dragons

In therapy, I learned to forgive my dad and release the past. I also discovered he criticized *in me* what he feared *in himself*. We are all on a course to do the same to others if we don't wrangle our own fearful Dragon into submission.

As a parent, friend, or co-worker, you are a Force at Work in others' lives. You will position yourself as an ally or an adversary, depending on how you respond to their dreams.

As Forces at Work, we manage fear — for ourselves and others — by setting it aside and exploring possibilities with curiosity and love. Sometimes it may be appropriate to offer feedback or point out inconsistencies, but we help others the most when we listen and lend them our belief in their potential.

Reflection

What is the Dragon telling you? What does your Dreamer whisper? What or who do you need to forgive and release? Whose dreams do you support?

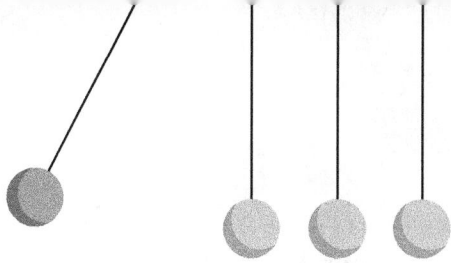

CHAPTER 7

this is no time to be realistic

Don't look for your dreams to come true.
Look to become true to your dreams.

— Rev.Michael Beckwith

I f you have a big vision, you are in good company. History is crowded with examples of ordinary people who had extraordinary visions.

Heroes like Martin Luther King Jr., Nelson Mandela, Mahatma Gandhi, Thomas Edison, and Joan of Arc all had big visions that existed in their minds before anyone else saw them.

In *Breaking the Habit of Being Yourself,* Joe Dispenza shares his own list of history's giants and observes: "These people all believed in a future destiny that was so real in their minds that they began to live as if that dream were already happening. They couldn't see, hear, taste, smell, or feel it, but they were so possessed in their dream that they acted in a way that corresponded to this potential reality ahead of time."[11] They behaved as if what they envisioned was already a reality.

But none of their visions were realistic in their time. Other examples of unrealistic achievements include inventions like our cell phones and air travel. None of the modern conveniences we take for granted now seemed realistic when they were first envisioned. Even the guy who originally suggested we put wheels on our suitcases got laughed out of the boardroom.

When you nurture your own compelling vision, you will see it clearly before everyone else does, and it will probably not feel realistic. And really, what has your commitment to being realistic ever done for you besides keep you playing small and waiting for a better time to act that will never come?

As crazy as it sounds, most of us could benefit from being a little more unreasonable. Often a new client will timidly share their dream with me during our first session.

> **As crazy as it sounds, most of us could benefit from being a little more unreasonable.**

They inevitably ask, "Do you think it's realistic?"

I always respond, "I certainly hope not!"

What Feels Big to You?

Karrie Kitch was doing it all. When I met her, she was the board chair for Erin's House, a center for grieving children.

She was also a bank vice president, a career in which she had spent more than 20 years. She was married and raising four children. Not only was she revered and respected professionally, but she was also doing important and rewarding work through her contributions and strong leadership on the board.

Under Karrie's leadership, their fundraising efforts created a significant surplus in the operating budget. Karrie and her executive director, Deb Meyer, wanted the full participation of the board to consider bigger possibilities, so they asked me to come in and do a visioning session with them.

This was the first time I met Karrie in person, and I remember feeling a little intimidated. Karrie struck me as supremely confident and extremely capable, so I was a little surprised when, after the event, she inquired about personal coaching.

As I listened to her story, I learned that Karrie's dream was not to continue her path in banking. Karrie wanted to retire early from the bank and become the CEO of her own household. When she shared that she and her husband had already figured out the financial piece, I was even more curious about why she wanted a coach.

Her biggest challenge was managing the emotional uncertainty of leaving a career that had defined her for more than 20 years. She could not imagine what it would be like to go from having every minute of her day choreographed to having complete freedom and flexibility in her days. Though she longed for a life unstructured by her corporate schedule, the prospect daunted her. She did not want to leave without a plan.

Karrie and I worked together during the last six months of her banking career. We revisited her purpose, creating a compelling vision for her new life that included running marathons, long weekends at the lake, extended time with each child, and more quality time with her husband. She wanted to bring the same dedication and commitment to her home that she had given to her career. As we talked, the picture became clearer.

I hear a version of this desire from many clients who come for coaching. Not all are ready to redefine their work as drastically as Karrie did, but many are tired of being goal-setting champions, always reaching for more, and prioritizing productivity above all else. They long to step off and get on a slower, smaller bus.

Like Karrie, they are looking for more time to enjoy life. They no longer want to sacrifice the present moment for the hope of a better one in the future.

THINK BIGGER

When it comes to your vision, bigger is better. I am not talking about bigger in the sense of scaling or having to become larger than life or doing more things. I am talking about what feels big to you. I am talking about your deepest, "if I won the lottery," seemingly most unreasonable desires. What would feel like a dream come true to you?

> What would feel like a dream come true to you?

My husband and I recently rewatched the NBC series *Parenthood*. I loved this show the first time I watched it while growing my business and raising a young family. I could relate to many of the strong female characters depicting this stage of life. Ten years later, I found myself relating more to the matriarch of the family, Camille.

Camille is always on her way to the backyard to tend her garden or sit by her painting easel. She volunteers a few hours a week at a food pantry and seems perennially available when her children or grandchildren need a heartfelt conversation or a freshly baked cookie. At the end of almost every episode, I sigh, murmuring, "I want to be Camille." My husband laughs because Camille and I couldn't be more different.

But for me, Camille represents a desire I have for a slower, more meaningful approach to life. Never hurried, she takes time to rest and be creative. She serves her community and is present with her family. However, she is also retired. I know I'm not ready to go full-out Camille, but I have identified the specific elements for which I was longing.

Creating a compelling vision means talking about your most closely held dreams and desires in specific terms before you taint the picture by being realistic. It is a heart exercise more than a head exercise.

I used to believe my dreams were only possible if I could see all the way to the end and know how I was going to reach them. Now I recognize how this limits me because sometimes the strategy is not immediately evident. Remember, we don't need to solve tomorrow's problems with today's resources.

In my case, my dream isn't more money, a bigger house, or a fancy vacation (although I'm open to all of them!). It is freedom. I want the freedom to learn and grow in the ways that matter to me; I want freedom in my schedule, and I want the freedom to create a career that only requires me to be loyal to my own truth and agenda.

We each have a unique dream and vision to work out in our own lives. Steven wants the freedom to create and lead from his heart in a place where he is celebrated and not just tolerated. Anousheh wants to explore. Melissa wants an adventure through which she can contribute her expertise on a world stage, and Karrie wants to nurture her family as a professional homemaker.

Most of us stay stuck in our current reality simply because our time, attention, and resources are wrapped up in it. It seems obvious, but redirecting attention and resources to your compelling vision will bring it into focus.

Imagine a teeter-totter with two baskets: one for your current reality and the other for your compelling vision. You've been putting all your "apples" (energy, effort, and attention) in the current-reality basket. Meanwhile, the basket for your compelling vision remains empty. It won't carry any weight until you start putting more "apples" there.

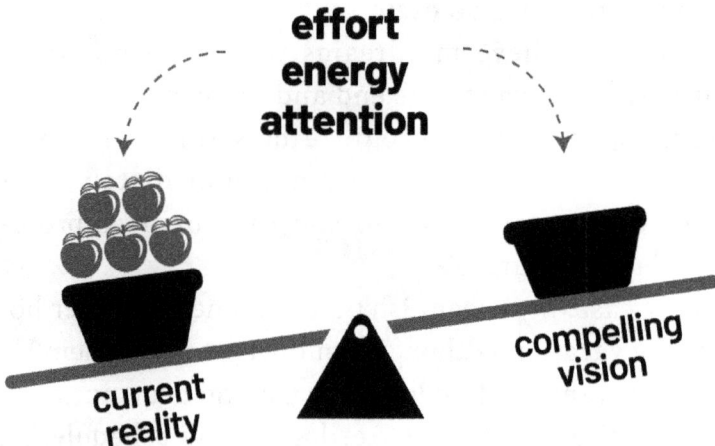

**effort
energy
attention**

current
reality

compelling
vision

Which are you nurturing, your current reality or your compelling vision?

Take Your Motivational Temperature

An effective way to evaluate the "bigness" of your unique dream is to check your motivational temperature. Our motivation level almost always relates to the quality and originality of

> The more authentic the vision is, the more motivated you will be to accomplish it.

our vision. Copying someone else's vision isn't going to cut it. The more authentic the vision is, the more motivated you will be to accomplish it.

THREE LEVELS OF MOTIVATION

In his book, *You Can Have What You Want*, Michael Neill identifies three levels of motivation.[12] They are desperation, rationalization, and inspiration. When I work with my clients, I explain these levels like this:

Desperation is the lowest level but is also remarkably effective because it engages our fight-or-flight survival response. You can tell you are in desperation mode if you use phrases like "I have to," "I need to," or "I must." It feels like there is an imaginary gun to your head, and catastrophic consequences will ensue if you do not reach your goal. Motivation by desperation turns you into a frantic ball of stress and is no fun for the people around you. It is also not sustainable.

Rationalization is the next level of motivation, and you know you are here when you encounter the word "should." This type of motivation ultimately means you are not taking personal responsibility for yourself and what you really want. You are holding yourself to someone else's standards. Rationalization as a form of motivation is tedious and perfunctory. An example might be, "I should go to church" or "I should exercise."

Inspiration is the highest form of motivation. Inspired by a vision of who you could be and what becomes possible if you act on your dream, you simply do what you *want* to do and trust it will take you in the right direction.

Win the Lottery

What is your big vision for your life? What is the desire that burns just below the surface? What might not appear big to anyone else but would mean everything to you?

I have some dear friends I've known since middle school. Dianne, Tari, and I have been supporting, challenging, and encouraging each other since big hair made its debut in the 1980s.

We recently rented a condo in Destin to celebrate our fiftieth birthdays. While we were there, the conversation turned to what we wanted for the next season of our lives. We each had lofty ideas but were having difficulty getting started on them.

I shared with them how I felt like I was trying to fly a little plane that was struggling to get off the ground because of the weight of everything it was holding. The idea for this book was already percolating, I was teaching leadership courses, and I had a full slate of clients. As we talked, I had an idea. I suggested an exercise to help us get past the block of our current responsibilities and see a bigger vision.

That night, we each bought a lottery ticket. We set them on the table, and before the winning numbers were drawn, each of us journaled about what we would do if we won the exact amount of money in the current lottery. (Spoiler alert: We did not win the lottery.)

Just before the drawing, we gathered in the living room and took turns sharing how we would spend every dollar if we won. There was something magical about having a specific amount of money to spend on our dreams that made them more tangible.

We imagined we would buy new homes for our parents and villas for each of us in Italy. Each of us had a foundation we would start for a specific cause we cared about. I would buy businesses for my kids to run. As we talked about it, our excitement level grew.

After a while, Tari remarked, "You know, many of these things are within our reach if we really wanted to work for them." I agreed. I know someone who just bought a home for her parents. We all knew someone who had started a foundation. Come to think of it, one of my favorite coaching mentors had just purchased a home in Italy.

We recognized that the things we wanted to purchase correlated with the values we wanted to honor — caring for our parents, supporting our kids in their dreams, serving our communities, and taking ridiculously great care of ourselves as we age. All were things we could do right now without winning the lottery.

We each wrote out goals inspired by our fully funded vision and committed to one action step we could take immediately. As my first action step, I wrote a check for $1000 to a charity that

> Instead of waiting for a time when you can do more, ask yourself, "What can I do *right now*?"

supports kids in foster care, something I care deeply about.

Instead of waiting for a time when you can do more, ask yourself, "What can I do *right now*?"

CHALLENGE

Grab a friend and buy a lottery ticket for each of you. (Please play responsibly.) Write down the amount of the current jackpot. Then, write out exactly what you would do if that amount was deposited in your bank account tomorrow. Share your thoughts and observations with your friend. You can share them with me, too, by joining the Forces at Work Community on Facebook.

Reflection

What is the highest and best vision you can imagine for your life if the vision were fully funded? What did you learn about your deepest desires through this exercise? What part of this is already within your reach?

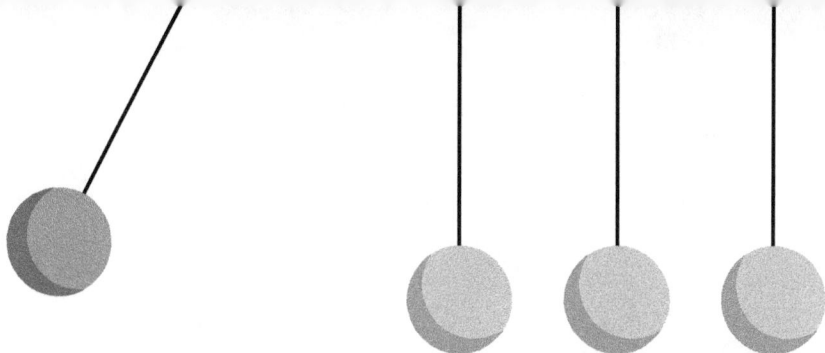

PART 4

develop
high agency

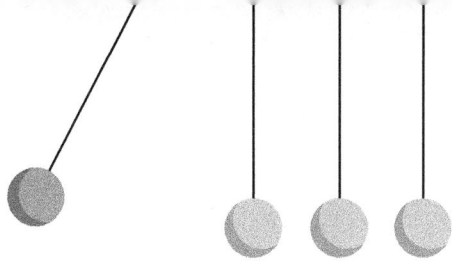

CHAPTER 8

a force to be reckoned with

What I am looking for is not out there. It is in me.

— Helen Keller

When my middle child, Grace, turned four years old, we held a birthday party for her in my makeover studio. Conveniently, its everyday decor already made it look like a pink dream, so when Adam added the final touches of birthday streamers and balloons, it was perfect! I got out the mirrored trays, the sparkly eye shadows, and the lip glosses. Amidst makeovers, games, and birthday cake, squeals of delight filled the house as we turned Grace's little friends into princesses for a day.

Watching her open her presents and play with her friends on her birthday was pure joy. And yet, I was worried. Even though Grace looked like a picture of health, I couldn't shake the feeling that something was wrong.

She had been having bloody noses.

They were alarming. I pushed past my shock each time I saw the bright red stain on her pillowcase by remembering that my older brother Andy used to get them. Maybe it was hereditary.

But then there were the fevers. Always low-grade, but almost always present. Together, the fevers and bloody noses felt like clouds gathering for a storm.

I talked to her doctor. He explained bloody noses were common and so were low-grade fevers. He assured me there was nothing to be concerned about. I had to agree she seemed fine, but I was still uneasy.

I took her back to the doctor several times that summer. Up until then, I wasn't the mom who brought her kid to the doctor for every little thing. But in a few short months, that is who I had become. Once for a cough, again for what turned out to be bug bites on her arm, and then for a regular checkup. At these appointments, the doctor always reminded me of two things: He had been a pediatrician for over forty years, and he had seen it all. She was fine. The conversation with him always felt a little patronizing, and I felt like a nuisance.

But the fevers and the bloody noses continued, showing up like unwelcome visitors who knocked at random times and rang the doorbell of anxiety at all hours. I was on high alert.

Shortly after Grace's birthday, we were playing on the floor. She was lying on her back, curved in front of me. I tried to get her to lie straight, but the curve was noticeable. I asked Adam to look at her.

"It doesn't look right," was all he said, looking at her abdomen. That was all I needed for the lead brick of dread to drop back into my stomach and for my determination to kick into overdrive.

GETTING ANSWERS

The next day, our little family drove back to the pediatrician's office together.

When we got to the clinic, our regular pediatrician was not there, so we saw a resident. At first, this discouraged me, but it turned out to be for the best. She was the first person to listen to all my concerns and complete a thorough exam.

I didn't know whether to be relieved or scared when she agreed the curve was troubling and added that Grace's abdomen also seemed distended. After a lengthy exam, she felt Grace must be constipated, so she wrote out a prescription for some MiraLAX.

We gathered up the kids and headed to the reception desk. They had added us to the schedule at the end of the day, so only the resident and the receptionist remained with us at the office.

I was on my way to teach a skincare class across town and had already shifted my attention to getting there on time. But as we opened the door to leave, the resident came into the lobby.

"Wait," she said. We all stopped and waited for her to speak. She seemed uncertain. "I am going to order an X-ray. I just want to make sure we got it right."

We almost didn't go for the X-ray. I figured she was doing it more to appease my nerves. Because she was a resident, I worried she would face additional scrutiny for adding a test my regular doctor had deemed unnecessary.

But at the last minute, we decided Adam would take the two kids over to the imaging center, and I would go on to my skincare appointment. Time was tight. We were leaving for vacation the next day and had already packed our bags.

After I returned home that night, Grace crawled into our bed and cried in her sleep all night long. Now she was clearly in pain. I didn't sleep at all. I went from unease to full- blown terror.

At 7:45 the next morning, the resident called. Adam had gone into work for the morning, and I was loading the car for our trip.

"We found a soft-tissue mass on Grace's kidney," she said.

The word "soft" sounded innocuous and shielded me from the full reality of what was about to happen.

She continued, "When you get back from your vacation next week, we'll set you up for an ultrasound to find out more. We will likely have to schedule a surgery to remove it."

"How big is it?" I asked.

"About the size of a softball," she replied calmly.

I knew right then there was no way we were taking this tumor with us on vacation.

I left my son Alec with a neighbor and called Adam as I drove Grace to the hospital. Our packed suitcases were still in the back of the van when I got there. We were going to need them.

During the excruciatingly long ultrasound, Grace fell asleep. My panic rose with each moment of silence. This was in the same tiny room where I'd come before to hear a heartbeat for the first time and watch a baby's first movements in the womb. It never occurred to me that an ultrasound could evoke so much anxiety and dread. I could hardly breathe.

After what felt like hours, I finally said to the young tech, "I need you to tell me what you see."

Visibly upset, she replied in a shaky voice, "I really can't. I have to call the radiologist, and they will talk to you."

The radiologist arrived and greeted me with a friendly, reassuring smile before turning to study the images. Grace was still sleeping. Eventually, the radiologist turned back to me and calmly said she needed to schedule surgery to remove the tumor immediately.

She made a few phone calls, and within minutes, two surgeons met me outside the ultrasound room. One told me they would schedule the surgery for the next day or the day after at the very latest. The other surgeon explained they would have to remove her kidney, too. It would be a complex surgery, so they would do it together. I couldn't believe it. My head spun, and I leaned on the wall for support.

Adam arrived shortly after, and we got scheduled for an MRI. While in the waiting room, we watched Grace twirl in the same purple dress I'd bought her for her birthday a few weeks earlier. I felt scared and helpless, swept away in an overwhelming tide of hospital processes and protocols. A nurse I hadn't met yet approached me with a clipboard. She held a device in her hand and said words that sounded like she needed me to sign for Grace to have a second surgery to install a port for her chemotherapy treatments.

"This is a mistake," I stammered. Everyone in the waiting room could hear the conversation. "My daughter doesn't have cancer. She has a tumor — a soft tissue mass, and they are going to remove it tomorrow." I honestly thought she had mistaken me for someone else.

She gently asked me to step into the hallway with her.

"I am with the pediatric oncology department. Grace has an aggressive cancerous tumor," said the nurse, not holding back. "She is going to need chemotherapy and probably radiation immediately after her surgery. If you sign this now, they may be able to install her portacath tomorrow when they remove the tumor, and we won't have to schedule a separate surgery."

In the next 48 hours, Grace underwent more tests, prods, and pokes than most people endure in a lifetime. During that short time, the tumor on her kidney doubled in size, growing as big as a football before they removed it.

DRAWING A LINE

At first, Grace handled things well. Except for her birth, she'd never been in a hospital. She complied helpfully with the nurses' requests. Two of her closest friends had arrived, bringing "get well" balloons and toys. The girls laughed and giggled as they played on the hospital bed, pushing the buttons to move it up and down.

But by the end of our second full day in the hospital, her energy began to wear thin.

As we settled in for the night, a doctor determined she needed an enema before her surgery in the morning. This would be the first really horrible thing she would endure, and it would leave a terrible memory.

"Trust me, you don't want to be here for this," the nurse said knowingly. "You can come back in when we are done and be the good cop."

I reluctantly stepped out of the room.

When I returned a few minutes later, Grace was lying perfectly still on the bed, her eyes fixed somewhere in front of her. She was completely despondent and silent, and I immediately regretted leaving her alone. I lay down next to her and stroked her hair. For the longest time, she didn't say anything. Then, assuming I didn't know, she told me what had happened.

I fought back my own tears and struggled for words. "I am so sorry. They are trying to get you ready so they can take this tumor out of you and make you better," I explained.

She turned around and looked into my eyes. And then a stronger version of her voice I'd never heard said, with steely resolve, "No one is ever going to do that to me again."

I believed her. In the chaos and fear of what must have been an overwhelming and powerless situation for a four-year-old, Grace had found her boundary and was drawing a line.

I was still scared but oddly proud of her in that moment. I realized that until then, my priorities had been to defer and be polite to every medical specialist who entered our space. At that moment, I knew I could not allow my fear of being a nuisance to get in the way of advocating for my daughter.

Grace's act of agency set the tone for what was to come. She was ready to fight, and she was going to be a force to be reckoned with. Our sweet baby would grow up way too fast over the next few months, but fierce resolve and strength would weave themselves into her personality, and we would learn about agency together.

The experience tested all of us. Within hours of her surgery, a nurse in a hazmat suit administered Grace's first dose of chemotherapy. Two days later, they sedated her again for her first radiation treatment. She would undergo daily sedation for two weeks. During that time, she lost 25 percent of her body weight. We shuffled back and forth from the ICU to radiology, to oncology, and back to her room on the children's ward. We were inundated with visitors who meant well. After the hospital released us to go home, we would return almost weekly for six months of chemotherapy treatments. Several times, I stood like a wall between Grace and a pair of scrubs declaring she had had enough for one day.

Our story has a happy ending because Grace is now all grown up, and although she is down one kidney, and we joke that she glows in the dark from all the radiation she endured, she is alive and healthy. Wise beyond her years, she is both kind and fierce, and she displays uncommon empathy for others. She is married to the love of her life. Earlier this year, she gave birth to our granddaughter, a true miracle.

Building Agency Expands Your Purpose

Of course, I think all the concepts in *Forces at Work* are important. But if I had to pick only one concept to incorporate into your life, it would be agency. I like to think of agency as donning a uniform that gives me permission to show up for myself and for others with confidence and authority, unapologetically bringing my ideas and processes into the world.

As such, agency is the degree to which we act independently, ask for what we want, and make our own free choices about how we live our lives. And it takes courage — especially in an age of experts and gurus.

Until I went through Grace's cancer journey with her, I lacked agency in many ways. I could point to many reasons for this, including my childhood and, in part, my religious upbringing. Each of us has our own unique obstacles on our path to agency. Advocating for my sick child was the first step to reclaiming the agency I lacked as a child and a young adult. It is amazing what we can do for someone else, even when we have failed to do it for ourselves.

Agency begins with setting physical boundaries, like Grace did in the hospital, but it's much more than that. It is also listening to your own intuition and discerning your best path in any circumstance.

> Agency is the degree to which we act independently, ask for what we want, and make our own free choices about how we live our lives.

building agency expands our influence

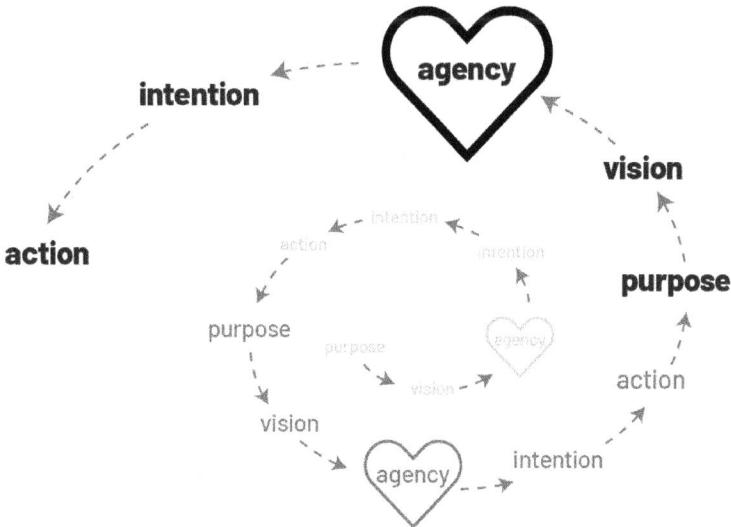

Agency is giving yourself unilateral permission to show up with confidence and authority, unapologetically bringing your ideas and processes into the world. The more you do this, the more your purpose expands. This is not a linear, one-time process. It is cyclical. In each cycle, you learn, assimilate new information, and grow. Your purpose grows stronger, your vision gets bigger, and your agency keeps growing to support it. You set stronger intentions and take on bigger actions.

With agency, you have authority over *how* you navigate your challenges. Developing agency is your personal responsibility; no one else can do it for you.

> With agency, you have authority over *how* you navigate your challenges.

Reflection

What thoughts came up as you read about agency? Do you tend to go along with the program, or are you more likely to question the status quo? What would it look like for you to develop more agency over your life or career?

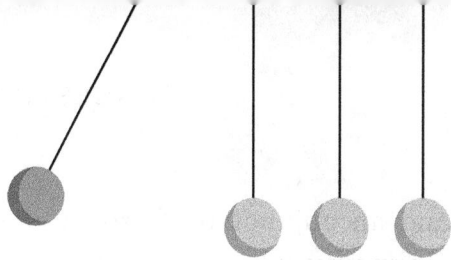

CHAPTER 9

do what you want

"One who believes in himself has no need to convince others."

— Unknown

No one has taught me more about agency than Bob Goff, and that is why I asked him to write the Foreword for *Forces at Work*.

Bob's first book, *Love Does*,[13] was published in 2012 and quickly made it to the *New York Times* bestseller list. His message resonated in the hearts of millions of readers, who he encouraged to jump into action and live audacious lives. Bob uses the proceeds from his books to fund his non-profit, Love Does, which helps fight injustice around the world, providing education for children in Uganda, Somalia, Nepal, Iraq, India, Congo, and Afghanistan.[14]

An accomplished attorney, Bob is also the Honorary Consul for the Republic of Uganda to the United States and an adjunct professor at Point Loma and Pepperdine University, where he teaches a class on failure.

Bob has an enormous sense of purpose and an even grander vision. Living by example, he empowers others to embrace their purpose and has created a movement of "doers" who are significantly impacting the world.

Bob is also known for his open-hearted assistance. When I asked him to write the foreword to *Forces at Work*, he immediately, generously, and enthusiastically agreed. Not because of who I am — an unknown author — but because of who he is and what he believes about himself and his role in the world. He did ask to read the manuscript first!

No matter the size of the crowd in attendance when he speaks, Bob gives out his personal cell phone number so people can reach him. If he can take a call, he will. *However, he can just as easily and without apology let your call go to voicemail.* Comfortable with his own agency, what he gives, he gives freely, and when he has other priorities, he doesn't feel obligated to answer.

I've adopted this philosophy in my own coaching. I welcome clients to call me outside of their scheduled sessions without fear of bothering me. This works out well if they understand my personal boundaries are

> People with high agency do what they *want* to do without second-guessing or guilting themselves into acts of martyrdom.

in place, and I may not take the call. But often, I do, and it is just what they need in the moment to move forward in a specific situation. People with high agency do what they *want* to do without second-guessing or guilting themselves into acts of martyrdom.

In *Love Does*, Bob shares a pivotal story about agency that changed the course of his life.

Bob did not get accepted to law school because he didn't have good enough grades. Instead of giving up, he showed up to the campus every day and sat on a bench outside of the dean's office until the dean finally told him to go buy his books and allowed him into the program. Bob's brave act of agency led to a life of phenomenal service and adventure.

We cultivate our agency one belief and one act at a time. One act of agency can change the course of your life, like Bob sitting on a bench until he got a yes.

People with low agency tend to respond to a closed door as if the story has already been written. When faced with what appears to be an ending, they go along with the role someone else has assigned to them.

In contrast, when the book shuts on people with high agency, they are more likely to pick up the pen and write their own chapter. High-agency people aren't afraid to challenge socially constructed realities that could keep them from reaching their potential.

Acts of agency can be small but significant. Setting boundaries,

> High-agency people aren't afraid to challenge socially constructed realities that could keep them from reaching their potential.

determining your schedule, and choosing how you spend your energy are all acts of agency. So is choosing how you dress, who you allow into your circle of influence, what you continue to do, and what you decide to quit. You express your agency by what you allow and what you tolerate. Every choice we make is an act of agency. With agency, you decide how you want to show up in the world.

High and Low Agency

In his book *Agency*, author Ian V. Rowe says, "Agency is learning to see ourselves not as victims of our circumstance, but rather as architects of our own better futures, and to do so even in the face of real obstacles." [15]

He also shares a report from the Archbridge Institute showing only 39 percent of American adults under the age of 25 think they have the power to live meaningful lives.

I am passionate about helping you grow your sense of agency. Without it, you're less likely to persevere when someone challenges you. As you pursue your biggest dreams, circumstances will always arise to cause fear, doubt, and uncertainty. This is normal. We don't need to be surprised or discouraged when they show up.

Agency is the muscle we develop to persevere and embrace these challenges as opportunities to grow.

> Agency is the muscle we develop to persevere and embrace challenges as opportunities to grow.

How do you know if you need to build more agency? The biggest tell is inaction. Low agency feels like waiting. When we are overly dependent on others, we wait for someone to give us permission to follow our dream. We wait and hope for someone to recognize or choose us, and we wait for a time that won't inconvenience anyone. Another low-agency behavior is appearing to remain positive by using hope as a strategy. This rarely leads to purposeful action.

With high agency, we step into action, and we are not afraid to take reasonable risks.

Of course, we still want others to like us, but we don't depend on anyone's opinion, nor do we need their approval. With agency, we don't need to explain ourselves or play the role of the convincer. When we feel the need to explain our worth or our ability to contribute, we take a weak position. Think back to Bob and his law school experience. When Bob didn't get into law school, he didn't get whiny. He simply stated what he wanted directly to the person who could make it happen, and he demonstrated his determination by backing up his request with action.

So how do we grow this magic power, and what are the obstacles to our agency?

Beware of Limiting Beliefs

If you are experiencing low agency in any area of your life or career, the first step is to examine your current beliefs. No beliefs are neutral. Your beliefs are either moving you forward or holding you back. Because your behavior will always follow your belief, choose to nurture beliefs that support agency.

In his book, *You Can Have What You Want,* Michael Neill reminds us that an elephant tied to a stake as a baby will remain captive for the rest of its life, even though, as an adult, it could easily break away from the tether. "Of all the beliefs and stories we make up about how the world 'really' works, the most limiting ones are those that take several isolated incidences of failure and generalize them to mean that we will be unsuccessful in all areas of our lives for all time," he wrote.[16]

When you live in the shadow of your failures and doubt your own skills and abilities, you more easily defer to others' agendas. If you believe you are ill-equipped to travel your own road, you jump on someone else's bandwagon. Supporting others in their dreams isn't wrong, but if you do it because you are unwilling to take your own risks, you avoid your own growth and miss out on your best life.

Limiting beliefs become more powerful when you fail to challenge them, and they lead to a condition known as "learned helplessness." Arguing for seemingly harmless limitations, like, "I'm not a runner," "I can't sing," or "I can't do math," will keep you comfortably buckled into the passenger seat of your life. Because the truth is, you *could* do all these things if you wanted to.

For years, I said I couldn't run. I joked, "I couldn't run if someone was chasing me," or, "I can't even run to the mailbox." Often, we hide the limitations we argue for under a layer of humor or sarcasm. The truth was, running made me uncomfortable.

After reading about learned helplessness, I decided to run. I downloaded an app that promised to take me from my couch to a 5K. At first, it was a lot of walking interspersed with short bouts of running. Within a few weeks, I built up some endurance and was surprised at how far I had come. It was incredibly empowering. I still don't love to run. But I no longer tell myself *I can't* do it.

When we fall back on excuses and spend energy explaining all the reasons we can't do what we really want to, we become experts at arguing for our limitations. This is a powerful form of self-sabotage. We will rise to the level of what we hear our mouths speak.

> We will rise to the level of what we hear our mouths speak.

Furthermore, by affirming these beliefs, we also affirm our position as passive spectators in our lives. Low agency is a thinking habit.

When you say things like, "I'm a procrastinator," "I can't handle conflict," or "I lack motivation," you are literally arguing for your limitations. If you want to change this, only allow yourself to argue for the limitations you want to keep — and if you think about them, are any of them really worth arguing for?

Agency Influences Action

Sometimes people who feel miserable in their careers don't make a switch because they fear "starting at the bottom," but this is a negative assumption. High-agency people don't approach a new experience by starting at the *bottom*; they approach it by starting at the *beginning*. Their reservoirs of experience, skill, and maturity will accelerate any learning curve they encounter.

When I met Sarah, she had been ambitiously dissatisfied with her high-paying job for more than 15 years.

Every year was another investment in a life she no longer wanted, but the thought of starting over at the bottom somewhere else appealed even less. This underlying belief was keeping her stuck. In our first sessions together, we uncovered her deeper purpose and talked about a more compelling vision for her life. She wanted to be an independent consultant and deliver her expertise on her own terms. We had just begun our work, but aligning those first two elements was all she needed to decisively reclaim agency over her life. After our third session, she sent me the following text:

"Hit my limit. Quit my job. Went fine."

We hadn't discussed a plan to quit or how she would replace her income, which was significant. In a mild panic, I wondered how her husband would take this news. Would he be angry and blame my coaching?

But this wasn't the first time a client made a bold decision that left me both amazed and feeling like I might have to join the witness protection program.

Sarah *was* fine, just as she had told me. She secured a better job in less than a week. We referred to it as her "bridge job" because it took her out of a toxic environment and gave her time to work on her big dream, which was to start her own consulting business. In a moment of truth, she overcame her limiting belief and reestablished agency in her career.

Healthy, high-agency people are confident in their ability to learn and grow. They exude a humble authority, remain confidently optimistic, and don't hang on too tightly to their past achievements.

Choose Your Beliefs

To have a healthy sense of agency, we must become skilled at both challenging and creating our beliefs. I invite you, as a Force at Work, to adopt the following core beliefs:

> To have a healthy sense of agency, we must become skilled at both challenging and creating our beliefs.

1. I have a unique and important purpose to find and fulfill.
2. I am at exactly the right place, at exactly the right time, and I have everything I need to succeed.
3. I am exclusively in charge of my life and my outcomes.

Agency Requires Focus

One of the greatest threats to our personal agency is the number of distractions and shiny objects battling for our attention. Our modern world inundates us with information, opportunities, and entertainment. Like bugs to a light, our minds are drawn to experts on TikTok, blue checks on Twitter, and influencers on Instagram. If we don't set up boundaries, these voices can hijack our attention, cause us to second- guess our paths, and recruit us to their agendas.

When our mental energy is diluted or contaminated, we lose the power we need to build agency.

In his book *Deep Work,*[17] Cal Newport chronicles how our declining cognitive abilities are due to a lack of attention and focus.

Every time I give out my email address at a store or online, a little piece of my soul dies. Do you ever feel this way? I dread entering a sales funnel where I will inevitably be barraged by a constant daily drip of information containing answers to questions I didn't ask and offers for things I don't need.

In my quest for agency, the last thing I need is a daily email from Bed Bath & Beyond.

Our potential is unlimited. Our mental energy is not. I have come to resent the word "content," as it seems synonymous with clutter. Social media content has become the junk food of learning. I prefer a good book any day. Most book authors have spent long hours honing their ideas and distilling them into their most helpful and concise forms. For me, a book is a well-rounded, nutritious mental meal.

> Our potential is unlimited. Our mental energy is not.

Opinions, Persuasions, and Convictions

I used to love watching the news and almost felt like it was a responsible act of citizenship to stay informed. I've since stopped watching and invite you to try it, too. Currently, the news industry is not operating from a place of love and confidence. Since it disproportionately focuses on negative events, it feeds the voice of the Dragon in our collective experience. Furthermore, this is the first time in history we can know about every tragedy in the world in real-time. We aren't meant to carry it all or become personally involved in every disaster that strikes. As I learn about events, happenings, and the stories people discuss around me, I find it helpful to decide my level of involvement by categorizing my thoughts as opinions, persuasions, or convictions. Each of these warrants a different amount of my limited energy.

OPINIONS

An opinion is a loosely formed thought about something I've heard, but I am not invested in the topic enough to research opposing viewpoints or vet the facts. In this case, expressing my opinion is almost always a waste of energy. What does it add to the conversation? Do I really care about this topic, or am I participating to feel like I belong?

This was a news flash for me: I don't have to have an opinion about everything. Every opinion I hold has an energy price tag attached to it.

> Every opinion I hold has an energy price tag attached to it.

And most of my unqualified opinions are energy leaks. I have a friend who wears a bracelet to remind him to check where his energy is going. The bracelet says: "WAIST," which stands for "Why Am I Still Talking?"

PERSUASIONS

Unlike opinions, persuasions are relatively well-formed ideas on topics I care about. So, I'm willing to invest time and energy in learning about them. Global warming, political ideologies, and parenting styles fall into my persuasion category. I've done enough research to develop an educated viewpoint about how to approach these issues in my own life. I would share my persuasion with someone if they asked me about it. My rants about content and the news industry are examples of persuasions — more than an opinion and yet not quite a conviction.

CONVICTIONS

Convictions are ideas I am wholeheartedly invested in. Not only have I done the research, including the exploration of differing viewpoints, but I also allow this conviction to inform how I live my life, and I am compelled to share it with others. Convictions reflect purpose and deserve our best, undiluted energy.

One of my personal persuasions I find graduating to the level of conviction is the idea we can choose to make any decision from a place of love or from a place of fear. I have seen this dynamic play out in the lives of my clients and other people I care about, and I am ready to speak and write about it. I put energy into practicing it in my own life. I also offer what I've learned to others and seek a community of people who are applying this idea in their own lives and businesses. I am passionate about this topic and am troubled when I see the consequences of fear and insecurity affecting our lives and communities.

I can't tell you exactly how many opinions, persuasions, and convictions you can hold in all, but I can tell you the number isn't very high. To give your convictions the time and energy they deserve, you may have to excuse yourself from arguing for opinions and persuasions that are lesser priorities for you. My friend CJ says, "If everything is important, nothing is important."

When you distinguish your convictions from persuasions and opinions, you won't have to accept every invitation to an argument. Save your energy for the important ones.

Knowing your priorities also allows you to put on blinders and say no when you are invited to support other projects. Not everyone will understand or support you in this. A highly developed sense of agency protects you from well-meaning manipulators — and maybe those who aren't as well-meaning, who may call you complacent or employ other tactics when you choose not to support their causes with your time, energy, and focus.

With agency, you view a request for your time and energy as an invitation, never as a summons. You recognize your "no" doesn't diminish what is happening in the world or the importance of what others are doing. It only means you know what is for you and what is not. Ironically, the more agency you have, the more others will see you as a person of influence, and the more requests will come your way. If you need to be flattered, you will be tempted to say yes. If you are grounded in your purpose, agency will allow you to decline graciously without remorse or fear of missing out.

A Commitment Scale for Determining Priorities

To measure priorities, I use the following scale:

Level One: This is not my cause. It is someone else's idea, but I feel like I should go along with it.

Level Two: It would be nice if I could pursue this cause, and I love to talk about it, but as I look at my schedule and my resources, I'm not ready to put any real action or intention behind it.

Level Three: I really want to do this, and I am going to *try*.

This is the worst place to land. It is the liminal space between high and low agency, where we allow ourselves to care and to expend some effort — but we are not committed to getting a result. In this case, I share the timeless wisdom Yoda gave to Luke when he was helping him build his agency as a Jedi Knight: "Do... or do not. There is no try."[18] Consider moving back to a Two, or forward to a Four.

Level Four: I am reasonably committed to this cause. I have a plan; I've scheduled my benchmarks, and I have allocated resources to support me. Barring a catastrophe, I will complete this project.

Level Five: Whatever it takes. I am unreasonably committed to this cause. Like a mother who would run naked into a burning building to save her children, I don't care if anyone helps me or what anyone else thinks of me. The train has left the station, and there is no way I am *not* doing this.

When considering a new project, check in with your commitment level at the beginning. If it is not at least at Level 4, look for a more compelling use of your time and energy.

Reflection

Do you overexplain or need to justify what you want to do? Do you wait for someone else to change, help you, or give you permission before you can act? What opinions or persuasions can you let rest to find more focus for your true convictions? What are your Level Five priorities?

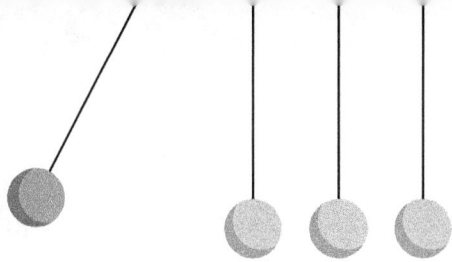

CHAPTER 10

harness the building blocks of agency

"Behavior follows Belief."

—Mary Lore

When I was a new coach, I volunteered to help lead a support group for people who were unemployed. Expectedly, most of the attendees were wrestling with financial uncertainty, anxiety, and discouragement.

One attendee, Clint, had been with the group for months. At one meeting, he shared he had interviewed with two different companies the previous week, and he had not received an offer from either.

"No one is hiring fifty-year-old men," he said, shaking his head.

I watched as the rest of the group sadly nodded and murmured in agreement. My first instinct was to do the same. Clint was obviously hurting. Maybe he just needed a safe place to vent.

But then, I realized that he could vent anywhere — and he probably was sharing this discouraging sentiment with anyone who would listen. I wanted to help him move forward.

So, I decided to take a risk and see if he would allow me to challenge his limiting belief.

"Clint," I said, "Is it really true that no one is hiring fifty-year-old men?"

He looked at me as though he heard words coming from my mouth but couldn't believe what I'd said. Until this point, I had allowed empathy, or maybe sympathy, to keep me from coaching more powerfully. But I knew if Clint continued to wallow in self-pity, he would be back again the next week with more stories of rejection. The rest of the group was staring at me now, and the room got quiet.

"What?" Clint said.

"You said nobody is hiring fifty-year-old men," I repeated. "Is it really true that nowhere in this big world is a fifty-year-old man accepting a job offer today?"

He stared at me but said nothing. I knew I was walking on thin ice.

"Clint, there are three things I know about belief." I walked up to the whiteboard and wrote these words:

1. There are no neutral beliefs.
2. Behavior follows belief.
3. We choose our beliefs.

"The story we tell ourselves about what is happening to us influences our outcome and our results," I said. "When we choose our beliefs from a place of fear and uncertainty, they work against us."

> The story we tell ourselves about what is happening to us influences our outcome and our results.

Then I added, "But when we choose beliefs from a place of love and confidence, they empower us."

At this point, I had clearly disrupted the meeting and thrown down a challenge. If I was going to help Clint and the others, I had to reposition myself as an ally and not an adversary.

So, I made a request: "Clint, would you allow me to challenge this belief and see if we can get you into a better head space today?"

He looked skeptical but nodded.

Tell a Better Story

My knowledge of managing belief comes from two great teachers. The first is Mary Lore, who wrote *Managing Thought*.[19] It is a textbook on getting your mind right, and I wish every high school psychology class required students to read it. The second is Byron Katie, who wrote *Loving What Is*.[20] She is widely credited with a series of questions that allow you to question and change your beliefs. The questions I asked Clint are based on her work.

Following her process, I intentionally wrote out Clint's limiting belief and repeated it numerous times. Too often, destructive beliefs slide into conversation without us noticing or challenging them.

I decided to start from the top.

"Clint, you said, 'No one is hiring fifty-year-old men.' Is that true?"

I saw the struggle on his face.

"It feels true, doesn't it?" I asked.

"Yes," he said. "I got two rejection letters this week, and I'm pretty sure those jobs went to people who are younger than me."

"So, it feels true, and you are telling yourself a story about who got the offers?"

"I guess so," he said reluctantly.

"Is it absolutely true? Can you know without a shadow of a doubt that no one is hiring fifty-year-old men?"

"Well, no, I can't say it is absolutely true," he admitted.

I continued.

"If we know that no belief is neutral, does this thought move you forward or hold you back? How do you feel when you think this thought, 'No one is hiring fifty-year-old men?'"

"Pretty helpless," he responded. And then he added. "Helpless, and... I feel washed up and like it's an unfair game. I feel ashamed that I am at this age and looking for work. I feel like a loser."

Now we were uncovering the energy behind the words. To honor the process, I repeated the belief again. "So, when you choose the belief that no one is hiring fifty-year-old men, you feel like a hopeless, ashamed loser playing an unfair game?"

"Yes," he said. And he smiled at the absurdity of it.

"What kind of energy do you think you are bringing to these interviews?" I asked quietly.

He laughed a little. "It probably seems a little desperate." He recognized.

Seeing that he was ready to move forward, I asked, "What if I could remove this thought from your brain? Thoughts are things, you know. What if I could reach into your brain and pull this one out?"

Eyebrows went up around the table. I continued. "What if this thought were no longer available to you, and you physically could not access it anymore? How would you feel if you could no longer think the thought, 'No one is hiring fifty-year-old men?'"

"I guess I would feel like I had as good a chance as anyone. I'd feel like I wasn't just going through the motions and showing up just to get rejected again."

"What else?" I asked.

"I would probably take more risks during the interviews and tell them more about my ideas and how my experience could help them. I would ask more questions and make sure they knew I was willing to learn, and I was ready for a challenge. I've thought about adding more technical skills to my resume."

He was turning a corner, and the energy in the room was shifting, too. Others were nodding their heads in agreement.

Ideas and suggestions began to flow. Even though the group was initially ready to commiserate with Clint, this was better. They would be much more willing to recommend him and network with him now than if they had continued to feel sorry for him.

We all hear echoes of this limiting thought, "I'm not enough." They sound like: "I'm too old/too young." "I'm not qualified enough/I'm *overqualified*." This shows how we can turn almost *any* characteristic into a positive or a negative attribute. Practice finding your positive attributes!

> **Practice finding your positive attributes!"**

The Three R's of Agency

In addition to telling a better story, here are three more elements we can nurture to build our agency.

RESILIENCE

Resilience is our ability to bounce back after a disappointment or a setback. We quickly challenge our stories and recognize beliefs that won't move us forward. As we do, our bounce-back time improves. Although we still may not like adversity, we begin to view it as an opportunity to build our agency muscles. Like Anousheh Ansari, we remain curious and committed to our goals. We look for perspective, being mindful of our emotions and not letting them have free rein. Resilience requires us to expect and prepare for setbacks as part of the process.

RESOURCEFULNESS

Resourcefulness is our ability to create new options so obstacles don't stop us. We find a way or make a way. When we are resourceful, we may request help, but we aren't waiting for someone else to "pick us" or "give us permission."

Writing *Forces at Work* was an act of agency for me. I wanted to write a high-quality, message-driven book to share my ideas with the rest of the world. I loved the idea of working with a traditional publisher, but I decided now wasn't the time to navigate all the ins and outs of that complex process. I also didn't want to write a cheaply done, self-published book that wasn't well organized. I found the team at Niche Pressworks, and they are providing me with an innovative solution. Here, I am able to publish with a high degree of professionalism and retain the rights to my book, keeping the door to traditional publishing open.

To be resourceful, we must think beyond conventional truth and socially constructed reality and create alternative options and paths for ourselves. What is your response when someone tells you it can't be done?

RESPONSIBILITY

If you are out of integrity with yourself, it is because, at some point, you stopped believing you had a choice about something and instead believed your only option was to compromise.

> If you are out of integrity with yourself, it is because, at some point, you stopped believing you had a choice about something and instead believed your only option was to compromise.

As a Force at Work, you accept that you are ridiculously in charge of your outcomes. You know you have choices — even if you don't like any of them. You recognize you don't "have to" do anything. When conventional paths don't serve you, you embrace self-guided education and find a new path forward.

Agency also means taking responsibility for the emotional trash in your yard, even if you didn't put it there. This might require going for counseling or therapy to heal past traumas and blocks. If you came from a home or a community that failed to help you establish agency, as an adult, you have the power and responsibility to do it for yourself. This doesn't mean you have to do it alone, but it does mean you are responsible for finding the resources and support you need.

You can build a high degree of agency, beginning right now.

High Agency and Healthy Detachment

"The courage it takes to leave behind what's not for you anymore is the same courage that will help you find your way to what is."
— *Cory Allen*

I am always surprised to meet highly successful people with low agency. In fact, some people lose agency when they become successful. It's the strangest thing. They allow their status, accomplishments, and achievements to hold them captive and rob them of their agency.

One of my favorite stories about Bob Goff is how he gave away his law practice. As his nonprofit, Love Does, began to take off, he wanted to put more of his energy and focus there. He no longer wanted to manage the firm he had built. Deeply driven by purpose and guided by a vision larger than himself, he resisted the urge to hang onto one of his life's biggest achievements that was also a valuable financial resource.

Bob didn't sell his practice. He gifted it to a partner who could continue to grow and develop it.

Bob could walk away lighter because his sense of agency was intact, and he knew new adventures lay ahead. The courage to walk away from what is no longer for us is the same courage that will launch us into our life's next chapter.

Reading about Bob's act of courage gave me the push I needed to give away my direct-sale business. It was a fraction of what Bob gave away, but my reason was the same. It had served its purpose for me, and turning over my customer base to my loyal assistant felt right. I would be free of it, she would benefit, and I knew she would continue to take great care of the customers I still cared about.

High-agency people travel light. They don't hang on to things that no longer serve their highest purpose.

> High-agency people travel light. They don't hang on to things that no longer serve their highest purpose.

Reflection

On a scale of 1–10, rate yourself in the areas of resilience, resourcefulness, and responsibility. What sad stories do you catch yourself repeating? What one action could you take to move closer to a 10 in each category? As you read about healthy detachment, what would you let go of if you believed you could?

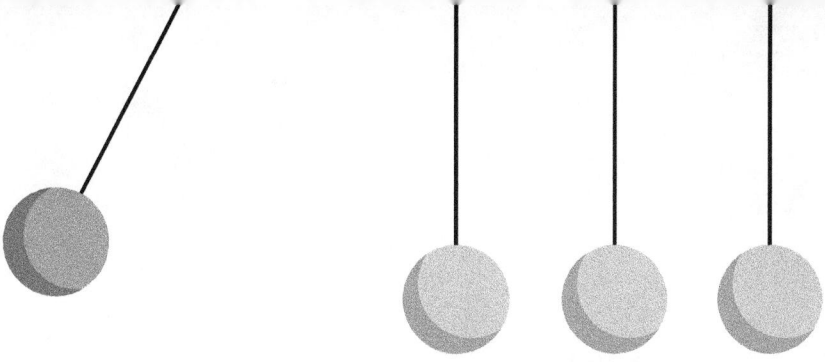

elevate your intentions

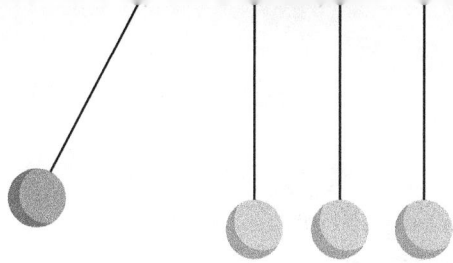

CHAPTER 11

discover your hidden intentions

"We get what we intend."

— Unknown

Kristi was a dedicated wife and mother and a high-achiev-ing, dynamic businesswoman. Just a few years after leaving her corporate job in marketing, she'd built a thriving business and was a sought-after consultant in her field.

Kristi loved owning her own small business, but she came to me because even though she enjoyed her work, it was becoming unmanageable.

She described how hard it was to get and keep clients and how much energy it took for her to keep the marketing funnel full of prospects. She could not stand the thought of losing a potential client and would go above and beyond her competition to secure business. She would bend over backward and compromise to secure contracts with clients whom she knew were not a great fit for her. She often shared that she had more clients than she knew what to do with, but she never let anyone go, and she continued to hunt for more.

Stopping for a quick breath in a flurry of words, Kristi briefly acknowledged her family was paying the price for her behavior.

"I mean, I'm doing it *for* them," she reasoned.

Kristi described how she would "fly in hot" to a school concert or a soccer game and, while there, would struggle to be present as the notifications on her phone lit up. And although she intended to be available for the kids after school, she almost never was. If they needed help with a school project, she found herself irritated and rushed to get through it so she could get back to work.

I asked her how she was taking care of herself. She described her intentions to walk and attend yoga. She told me in detail about how she used to run because she knew how important it was to stay in shape. But though she talked a great game about her past and future efforts to prioritize self-care, I noticed none of these activities were happening at present.

Digging a little deeper, I asked Kristi who supported her.

She replied her husband was her best friend and supporter, but recently they had their hands full, dividing and conquering the demands and responsibilities of three kids in school and extracurricular activities. Their dedicated date night had gotten swallowed up in parenting time. As she described their relationship, her affection for him was obvious, but their relationship also had the marks of a transactional business partnership.

Then I asked Kristi about her friendships. She admitted she was also neglecting them. "Good friends understand when you're busy, though, right?" she asked. Throwing her hands up, she added, "We are all just crazy busy."

Instead of prioritizing the relationships that nurtured and supported her, Kristi invested time with her business connections by attending industry events and conferences. She rarely declined for fear of missing an opportunity or losing her edge and becoming irrelevant.

As we talked, she seemed to hold nothing back. She was an open book, and I was learning a lot about her. For all her amazing qualities, what became clear to me was that she wasn't running her business; it was running her.

I noticed a pattern she had of articulating a problem and immediately justifying what was causing it. The more we talked about it, the more invested she became in her excuses, and I suspected she was looking for understanding, and maybe even approval, from me.

My first job was to interrupt the story Kristi was telling herself and help her face her misalignment honestly.

Remember the J-Curve? Kristi hadn't yet acknowledged the real cost of her behavior, and by asking questions, I was gently leading her to see the bottom of the curve.

We Can't Solve a Problem We Are Not Willing to Have

Behavior follows belief, and beliefs are born out of intentions. I was curious about the underlying intentions driving Kristi's behavior.

Intentions are the internal agreements we've made with ourselves that always produce our results. Often when I am debriefing with my own coach on a particular project, she will remind me, "Missy, based on your results, you got exactly what you intended." Of course, I celebrate good results, but if the results are adverse, I've learned to uncover my hidden intentions.

Because Kristi's behavior was clearly out of alignment with her stated values, it was time to find out what underlying intention was driving her. My friend Ellen, an insightful prosperity coach, author, and speaker, asks each of her clients to describe their first memory of money. In doing so, she helps them uncover the hidden intentions driving their work and beliefs.

> Intentions are the internal agreements we've made with ourselves that always produce our results.

My intuition told me this might help in Kristi's case, so I asked her to journal about her very first memory of money for our next session. This is the story she told me a few weeks later.

> When I was 9 or 10, we got a cat. I was over the moon. My grandparents had purchased two beautiful Persian kittens and gifted one to our family. They brought her to me during one of their rare visits that I remember. This dark-haired Persian beauty and I instantly bonded, and I fell in love with her. For several years,

it seemed she was my only companion and friend. I dressed her in doll clothes, snuck her into my bed, and she lay in my lap for hours at a time while I read. I named her Lyla.

Around that time, my dad retired from the military, and the structure that had kept him on course was gone. He was in his forties, and we endured months of unemployment and his consequent anger and depression. Sometimes he wouldn't leave his room for days, only to emerge in a rage, stomping through the house and yelling at whoever was nearby. My mom took the brunt of my dad's anger. Although he was never physically abusive, he was explosive, vindictive, and sometimes cruel. He eventually found another job, and our reprieve from anxiety came every morning when he left for work.

My parents' relationship settled into a cold war. My mom didn't work outside the home, so his primary way of controlling her was to withhold resources. Sometimes it was innocuous, like having the cable or the phone disconnected unexpectedly. At other times, it was more severe. Heat, food, and medical care were only available based on his good or bad mood, so my recurring ear infections and tooth aches often went untreated. If there were no groceries at home, sometimes he would eat dinner at a local diner on his way home from work, leaving my mom to scrape together what she could find to feed herself and us kids.

My mom didn't feel that leaving was an option, so her response to this treatment was to dig in and not let him win. When the heat went out, she found an electric blanket for me to sleep under. She scraped and saved everything she could and tried to stand in as a buffer to protect my brother and me from my dad's behavior.

I learned to be content with very few material comforts. When he was home, I stayed out of his way by tiptoeing around. I could spend hours reading quietly in my room with Lyla.

On top of my dresser sat a Ball jar partially filled with coins. I'm sure my dad had given me many of the coins for doing a chore here and there; he loved teaching me the value of hard work. Some of the coins were change from the birthday cash my grandparents would send. I would occasionally take out a quarter and ride my bike to Botners, a small store a few blocks away. I remember they had an irresistible candy counter filled with fizz candy, Charleston Chews, and Bubblicious gum.

One day, my mom came to my room and asked me for the money in my jar.

She told me she needed my coins to buy cat food and explained if we couldn't buy the food, we'd have to give Lyla away.

Without a second thought, I gave her all the money in the jar. I couldn't bear for Lyla to be hungry, and I was terrified of losing her. I couldn't imagine handing her over to a stranger.

After my mom left, I found Lyla and curled up with her on my bed. I looked across the room at the empty jar on my dresser. Panic struck me as the realization sank in. My money was gone, and I had no more to give.

A few weeks later, probably out of spite toward my mom, my dad gave Lyla away.

Devastated and angry, I tried to run away but only made it to the garage. I didn't have the resources to leave. This was the first time I remembered feeling utterly and completely powerless.

I decided I would do whatever I could to never feel that powerless again. I learned how to make money babysitting and doing chores around the neighborhood. When I turned sixteen, I worked two jobs during school and added a third in the summer. I even entered and won a local pageant, motivated solely by the prize money. During high school and college, I worked harder than anyone else and was applauded for it.

Hidden Intentions Can Wreak Havoc

Kristi hadn't thought about Lyla or the money jar in years. But now, she saw the intention that had been planted in her young heart that day and how it was driving her actions now. Her response to the powerlessness and loss of control she felt was to make money. In fact, her response to almost every situation was to make money.

Because the issue came from the financial lack of her early home life, Kristi easily internalized the three scarcity beliefs Lynne Twist identified: "More is better," "there is never enough," and "this is just the way things are."[21]

Kristi connected the problem of not having or being able to make money with a feeling of unbearable sadness and powerlessness. Money represented for her the control and agency she had lacked as a child.

Her little girl's mind had rationalized that if money was the one thing that could have saved her cat, she never wanted to be without it. If money could relieve the pain in her ears or fix her teeth, she would have it. If money could keep the heat and the cable on so her little brother could watch cartoons, she would find it. If money could calm her dad's anger and breathe happiness into her mom, she must figure out how to get some. Without resolving this wound, Kristi's inner child was going to keep calling the shots.

Money gives us choices, and a strong work ethic brings rewards — no one doubts these things. But earning money had become Kristi's supreme solution to every problem she faced.

Unfortunately, it would never heal the wound from her childhood. Money doesn't heal our trauma or our relationships, as hard as we might try. We can't solve an emotional problem with a financial solution.

If you remember Maslow's Hierarchy of needs[22] from high school psychology, Kristi appeared to be at the top of the pyramid, but her inner child remained stuck on the bottom rung. The trauma she had experienced made her feel there wasn't enough, and she needed to earn more. "Always be earning" was a powerful intention that squeezed out any time for self-care or nurturing relationships. It was a coping mechanism that protected her as a young person, but now it was making her life unmanageable, and she needed to let it go.

Recognizing that Kristi had some deep wounds from her past that were outside the bounds of a coaching relationship, I encouraged her to find a therapist to work through some of these memories. She began EMDR therapy, and we continued our coaching to support the changes she would make in her life and business.

In a short time, Kristi replaced her fear-based intention of "Always be earning" with one that came from a healed place of love and confidence: "Making money is fun and easy, and I always honor myself and my family first."

Less than a year after our initial discussion, she had completely restructured her life and her business around her true priorities. Before scheduling time for industry conferences, she planned family vacations. She reconnected with her closest friends and intentionally scheduled regular dinners and even a girl's weekend. She ended her workday by 3:00 p.m. so she could go for a run and be home when the kids got off the bus. The person showing up in my office still had a lot of energy, but it felt different. In place of the frantic, frazzled, over-caffeinated worker bee was a more settled, confident, and joyful woman.

The best part of Kristi's story is the ending. At the end of the year, while completing her annual financial review, she was shocked to learn that she had significantly increased her income. By choosing a new intention and only accepting clients and projects that fit with her intentions, schedule, and priorities, she allowed herself to work less, yet in doing so, she made more money, not less.

Intentions are like subway lines. We can select from endless choices and combinations. They lead to many destinations — none inherently good or bad. But whatever train we get on will take us to a specific destination. Just like on the subway, when setting an intention, you don't always see the way as you travel, but you know where you will end up. If we get on a train to the Bronx, we can't expect to end up in New Jersey.

Reflection

What intentions have been driving your behavior? What is it you want to avoid at all costs? Where do you find yourself stating one value but making excuses for not honoring it in your day to day? What new intentions do you want to create?

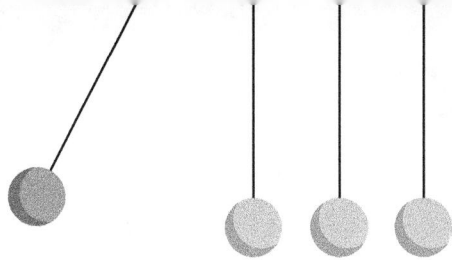

CHAPTER 12

be more than you do

"To be is a stronger foundation than to do."

— Robin Chaddock

Abandon Your Goals

I am not a big fan of goal setting, though I used to be. Ticking off a list of goals used to assure me I was doing OK. But as a recovering overachiever, I have a different perspective now.

What has changed is my understanding of intention. I learned this lesson alongside one of my favorite clients.

As a card-carrying overachiever believing in the almighty power of hard work, Michael couldn't understand why his business was struggling. As his long-time business coach, I couldn't, either.

In recent years, he had improved his processes and his team. He received most of his contracts by referral from current and past clients who were delighted with his service. It seemed he should be on the verge of a growth spurt, but instead, he was putting out fires and struggling to make payroll. The cost of a few large jobs came in way above his estimates, and as a result, he had become gun-shy about bidding on new work. To make matters worse, the IRS randomly audited his books, and the added pressure seemed unbearable. After several months with no reprieve from bad news, stress radiated from his body, and I worried about his health.

My intuition told me we needed to regroup and focus on Michael's personal health and well-being. Henry Wadsworth Longfellow famously said the best thing we can do when it is raining is to let it rain. Michael was in the middle of a deluge, and I wanted to find a way to support him until the storm passed.

At our next session, when Michael slumped down in the chair across from me and began delivering the latest chapter in the saga of "hard things," I gently interrupted him.

"Michael," I began, "I'm not sure why all of this is happening, but I think we need to break a cycle in your relationship with your business. Talking about the struggle week after week hasn't helped, nor have the strategies and solutions we've been trying to implement. I suggest we set the business issues aside for a few months and focus solely on who you want to be right now and how you want to show up for these challenges."

Relieved, Michael enthusiastically agreed, so I pulled out the personal goals we'd set earlier in the year. Michael wanted to do several things: run a marathon, spend long weekends at his lake house, make a significant contribution to his church, and, more than anything else, get his pilot's license.

At that moment, I recognized that Michael's personal goals were much more closely tied to his values than his business goals were. His personal goals clearly reflected how he wanted to show up for himself, his family, and his church community. They spoke to who he wanted to be more than to what he wanted to do. In that respect, they were more like intentions than goals.

For the next few months, Michael thrived in the space we had created, where he could take a break from thinking or talking about what was going wrong with the business. At each session, I resisted the temptation to ask how the business was doing. Instead, we dove right into his personal goals, and he lit up as he shared his plans and progress with me.

That year, Michael ran a marathon, and he also spent most of his weekends with his wife and kids at their lake house. Despite his own financial uncertainty, he donated funds to install a new sound system for the school attached to his church. And even though it took a lot of time and effort, he also got a pilot's license and his instrument rating.

That year, Michael's personal transformation was undeniable — he became the man he always wanted to be. Remarkably, the business turned around seemingly all by itself.

This demonstrates the power of aligning our internal world. When Michael honored and expressed his values, he got different results at work. He set boundaries, let go of the clients who haggled over prices, and dealt directly and definitively with the IRS issues. He hired new managers and joined a leadership training company to help support his employees with their personal and professional goals.

Today, Michael's business has grown beyond his wildest dreams, and more importantly, he is proud of the leader he has become.

The Problem with Goals

Goals are valuable and useful for us in our personal and professional lives but are not a perfect solution to every business issue. Here are some reasons why:

1. WITHOUT INTENTION, GOALS LACK POWER.

In his book, *Intention*, Andrew Wallas points out, "Goals are rational, logical, linear, task-oriented, and left-brain focused. They can be effective and bring about modest success, but in my experience, they are limited and frequently don't work." [23]

After years of coaching clients like Michael, this was my experience as well. Wallas suggests that goal setting is a left-brain activity, and because goals don't integrate the whole person, they often fail.

When we face resistance in pursuit of a goal, we must rely on the limited resources of willpower and discipline to white-knuckle our way over the finish line. Remember the tired rowers who've forgotten sailing is possible? This is that situation, and it is exhausting and unsustainable.

2. GOALS PULL OUR ATTENTION TO A POINT IN THE FUTURE, OFTEN DISCONNECTING US FROM THE PRESENT MOMENT.

If we are focused on the hope that we'll be better off when we reach our goal, we risk not enjoying where we are now.

Intentions help us define and practice *who we want to be* before *what we are going to do*.

3. GOALS ARE MORE PRONE TO EXTERNAL INTERFERENCE.

When we set a goal, there are always circumstances we can't control, and sometimes those circumstances affect our results on the scoreboard. In contrast, intention implies we have supreme responsibility for the lives we are creating. There is no scoreboard, but neither is there room to blame anything or anyone else for our experience. We don't fail; we only get results. We incorporate — even welcome — obstacles and resistance as lessons that help us grow stronger in our intention. From the outside, this looks like resilience and shows up as grit.

4. GOALS ALLOW US TO CONTINUE PRODUCING RESULTS WITHOUT A DEEP CONNECTION TO OURSELVES.

When I was in elementary school, I developed a knack for taking multiple-choice tests. In high school, my ACT chemistry score was above average, though I never studied chemistry. My score wasn't connected to my knowledge. I could keep taking those tests all day long, and it wouldn't change a thing. The dark side of goal setting can be a little like this.

Misalignment is inevitable when our goals keep us busy in a way that distracts us or even disconnects us from recognizing and honoring our deeper intentions. If we get lost in mindless achievements, we can lose sight of what really matters.

5. GOALS CAN MORPH INTO FEAR-BASED RULES.

Rules indicate that we need to be managed and that we can't trust our own behavior. This mindset directly opposes becoming a Force at Work who seeks to build agency. An example of a fear-based goal might be a daily calorie limit or a rigid exercise routine. Relying on superficial rules to manage our perceived weaknesses and shortcomings is a step in the wrong direction.

> Rules indicate that we need to be managed and that we can't trust our own behavior.

SIDE NOTE

If goals are fraught with so many problems, why does every business in America depend on them to measure progress?

Well, for starters, goals have that nifty, overused SMART acronym: specific, measurable, achievable, realistic, and time-bound. Secretly, we are all tired of it, but no one has yet created a clever acronym for setting intention. Perhaps that will be in my next book.

Also, goals are easy to measure. You don't have to do much deep work to know if you are hitting the target.

The Advantages of Intention

Setting intention has the power to transform, yet the mainstream business culture has not yet fully embraced it. This is because we Type A personalities love the linear, measurable results that goals promise.

Intention invites us to loosen our grip on control and trust the process. The greatest challenge with incorporating intention is that it moves us away from the certainty we crave when setting a goal.

At their best, goals and intentions work together. But for the sake of contrast, I want to share a comparison between a goal mentality and an intention mentality — because even though goals and intentions are both valuable tools, they feel very different.

> At their best, goals and intentions work together

143

Goal Mentality	Intention Mentality
Left-brained	Holistic; fully integrating mind, body, and soul
Marks progress	Draws us into meaningful process
Future-oriented	Brings power to the present moment
External measurements	Internal measurements
Relies on willpower, external pressure, and accountability	Relies on inner alignment, desire, and a higher power
Achieves	Creates
Stationary and fixed	Fluid and energetic
Defines what we want to do	Defines who we want to be
Relies on cognitive abilities	Trusts intuition
Knows	Feels
Starts and finishes	Grows and expands
Forces behavior	Prioritizes belief
Rowing	Sailing
Needs certainty	Navigates ambiguity
Feeds the ego	Supports the soul
Builds reputation	Builds character
Appeals more to our masculine energy	Appeals more to our feminine energy

Build Your Intention on Alignment

Remember when I shared how behavior follows belief? It is very hard to behave contrary to who you believe yourself to be. Through intention, we honor the truth of *who we are.* Our actions will follow naturally. Without intention, goals require constant rowing, and this takes a lot of external energy, strength, and brute force. Goals are good for quick starts and short distances. Setting intention, like sailing, requires more preparation and skill. But once the journey is underway, sailing will take us further, and we'll enjoy the journey more.

Goals require rowing. Intention prepares us to sail.

Shape Your Life with Intention

When I first recognized my business was desperately out of balance, one of the first intentions I set was for my work to feel "Fun and Easy." It was a big departure from my regular "work harder than anyone else and be responsible for everything" modus operandi. At first, it felt as ridiculous as it sounds, but the "Fun and Easy" litmus test ended up changing my life and my business for the better.

I had already noticed my most powerful client engagements *did* feel fun and easy to me. Helping clients like Steven, Melissa, and Michael gave me so much energy. Their issues and challenges were significant, but in all cases, we both immediately realized that what they needed was exactly what I was offering — namely, my Forces at Work framework. I gave myself permission to step out of strategic planning and accountability coaching, as both of those felt draining to me. I chose to work with clients who were hopeful and optimistic.

One Word

To end this section on intention, I want to share a powerful practice that can elevate your relationship with intention. It is called One Word.

I first learned about One Word through my personal trainer, who shared a video clip of Jon Gordon speaking about it. Jon went on to co-author a book about One Word,[24] and it has become a powerful movement today. The One Word concept has had more impact on my life than any other coaching tool I've encountered. Ever since learning about it, I've chosen a guiding word for each year.

Jon describes how he chose the word "purpose" as an anchor for the whole year. It allowed him to recognize and dismiss distractions that may have otherwise derailed him. It also allowed him to hang tough when he met challenges because he had determined in advance that his purpose was bigger than whatever problem he would encounter.

THE BENEFITS OF THE ONE WORD PRACTICE

The One Word practice offers many benefits:

1. **One Word brings significant character development, confidence, expertise, and depth.** One Word allows you to go deep and put down roots of

characteristics that matter to you. As you grow in your word, you become more interesting because you will have expertise and authentic experiences to share.

2. **One Word inspires actions and connections you would not have otherwise considered.** One year my word was peace. That year I learned about a woman who gave away all her possessions and changed her name to Peace Pilgrim. She walked thousands of miles for the cause of peace. She inspired me, and she is the reason I took on walking as a daily personal practice.

3. **One Word is a filter that can tip you off the fence when facing a hard choice. For example, "Which of these options will bring more peace into my life?"**

4. **One Word reinforces a positive vision of where you want to go this year.** It is a theme. A through-line. Of all the wonderful things you could measure this year, you have chosen one priority. You can look back one year from now and see how you have grown in this area instead of spending a little energy in a hundred other ways.

5. **One Word gives you flexibility with the how.** Two people might pick the word "generous" and have very different experiences over the course of the year. One Word keeps you grounded, but your creativity in how you grow in that word is endless.

FIND YOUR ONE WORD

Your word will find you. Set your intention to discover your word, and you will know it when you hear it. What do you want more of in your life right now?

This year, my word is "Elevate." Elevate feels very different from the year I chose the word "Slow." That year, I added more self-care to my routine — yoga, long walks, and unscheduled weekends. This year, I'm writing a book, developing a keynote, and expanding my coaching and retreat offerings. Choose a word that expresses what you want in your life right now.

By the way, there is nothing magical about picking a word in January or even for keeping the same word for an entire year. In 2019, when "Brave" felt complete for me, I adopted a new word mid-year. It was "Peaceful Growth." (So, you can even pick two words!) All that bravery had brought in so much new business, I needed to move into something that would help me stay grounded and balanced and not give up all the lessons I learned from Slow. My advice: Don't turn One Word into a rule. You can trust yourself to know when the lesson is complete and it's time to choose a new word.

Intention Builds Community

Before I learned about the power of intention, I held goal-setting workshops, at the end of which each participant left with a sheet of SMART goals. I've since abandoned those workshops in favor of my current practice of holding intention-based retreats.

Since I work with professionals who get pulled in a hundred different directions in December, instead of avoiding that month, I embrace it by holding the retreat for them then. It takes true intention to prioritize ourselves and attend a retreat in December, so I know these are my people!

The resort where we stay features condominiums with floor-to-ceiling windows facing the Gulf. While we are there, we prop open the doors, letting the ocean air surround us. At night, we fall asleep to the sound of the ocean waves. During the day, we meet in small groups, walk on the beach, and reflect on the year that is ending and plan for the new one ahead. We each choose our One Word for the coming year.

Then, on the last night, we order pizza, turn up the music, and we each use our One Word as an anchor to create our own vision board. I am always amazed to see these works of art become stunning visual representations of our intentions for the coming year.

Sharing these intentions and dreams with each other creates a powerful bond like none other. We stay in touch throughout the year to support and celebrate our growth. Those old SMART goals workshops I once held simply don't compare to this fully integrated experience of sharing deeply held intentions within a supportive and connected community.

Understanding, embracing, and setting intention prepares us for the next and most fun phase of becoming a Force at Work — taking inspired action.

Reflection

What is your initial reaction to the conversation about goals versus intentions? How can you prioritize who you are becoming over what you are accomplishing? What One Word would characterize what you want for your growth and development right now?

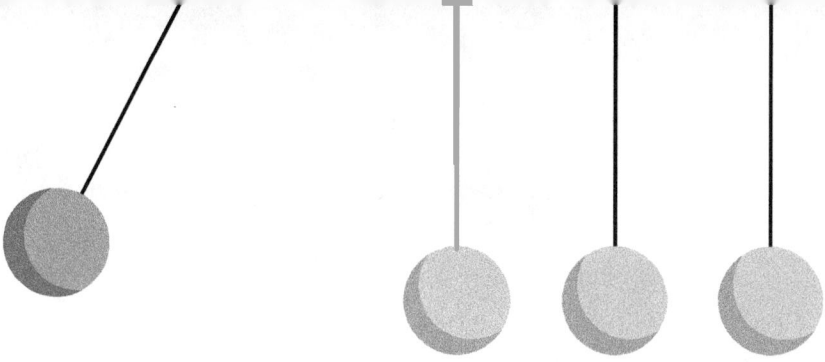

choose actions that ignite change

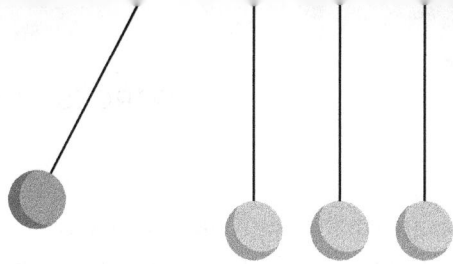

CHAPTER 13

a mile a day

"You often feel tired, not because you've done too much, but because you've done too little of what sparks a light in you."

— Alexander Den Heiger

By now, you can see how honoring the Forces at Work in your life — Purpose, Vision, Agency, Intention, and Action — can transform you into a Force at Work in the world. In this final section, I will challenge you to create inspired actions to practice moving forward in alignment.

Action invites experience, and our experiences transform us. For example, some of us share the common empowering experiences of learning to ride a bike or learning to swim. Do you remember the frustration you felt as you first struggled to stay afloat, followed by elation when you swam away from the

> Action invites experience, and our experiences transform us.

edge of the pool on your own? Or how powerful and capable you felt the first time you rode your bike to a friend's house by yourself? No one can really *teach* you these skills; you must *do* them. Not only do these accomplishments transform you — you *become* a swimmer, and you *become* a bike rider — but these skills also unlock greater freedom and open the door to even bigger experiences.

The goal of a purposeful practice is similar, only now you will be choosing *inspired actions* born out of your purpose and vision.

Dream Big, Start Small

On April 19, 1967, Kathrine Switzer rolled into Boston with several of her guy friends to run the Boston Marathon. The men were on the track team at Syracuse University. In the absence of collegiate sports for women, Kathrine had gotten permission to run with the men's track team during their practices. Yes, you read that right. As late as 1967, there were almost no collegiate sports for women.

During practice, the guys talked about running the Boston Marathon. Kathrine challenged them to quit talking about it and do it. So, along with Kathrine, they all registered for the race, piled into the car, and headed to Boston for the big day.

What makes this interesting is that no woman had ever run the Boston Marathon before.

When the group arrived for the race, the weather was cold and rainy. Kathrine wore baggy gray sweatpants, and for the first mile or so of the race, no one noticed she was a woman.

But that changed when the press truck came by and spotted her. A race official infamously jumped off the truck and attacked her, trying to pull off her numbers while screaming at her to get out of "his" race.

Reacting quickly, her boyfriend hip-checked the race official and sent him sprawling. Shaken but now even more determined to finish, Kathrine kept running. In that moment, she knew she had to finish the race for the sake of every woman who would come behind her.

There is a misconception about this story that Kathrine broke a rule and entered an all-male race. While the Boston Marathon had been an all-male race for 70 years, it wasn't because there was a rule against women participating. Something even more powerful was in place. Can you imagine what?

It was a widely accepted limiting belief. A modern-day myth.

In 1967, conventional wisdom held that women *couldn't* run long distances because if they did, their legs would get big, their uteruses would fall out, and they would grow hair on their chests. It seems ludicrous now, but this was the governing belief.

ONE SIMPLE PRACTICE CAN POWER A DREAM

So how was this twenty-year-old college student able to overcome a socially constructed reality and find the courage and confidence to attempt what most of the world believed was impossible?

I think it goes back to something that happened when she was 12 years old.

Kathrine wanted to join the field hockey team.

Since there was no middle school team, she would be competing against high school kids who were a lot older than her. She told her dad about this desire, and he gave her some powerful advice.

Parents, take note. He didn't point out that she should set a more realistic goal, wait a year, or even find something entirely different and "more realistic" for her.

He honored her desire. He held space for it. He also gave her an opportunity to develop agency by encouraging her to take one simple action: Run a mile a day.

Kathrine accepted the challenge from her father, and when it came time for the tryouts, she felt confident.

"I had a sharp sense of having accomplished something measurable and definable. I won a little victory every day that nobody could take away from me."[25]

She made the team. When Kathrine's dad encouraged her to run a mile a day, he was teaching her to make and keep an agreement with herself by using what I refer to as a daily purposeful practice. In this way, he helped her build confidence. He also helped her honor her desire, and he resisted the urge to make her justify it or to protect her from failure. He remained curious, leaving room for her to explore. He also didn't overindulge her or go overboard with assistance. He didn't buy her special shoes or hire a personal trainer.

He gave only the simple advice to "run a mile a day and see what happens."

Remember the Dreamer and the Dragon? They look inside your internal "filing cabinet" for evidence of your success or failure.

When considering a new desire, if your Dreamer looks and finds evidence that you can make and keep an agreement with yourself, it confidently leads you to take a bigger step next time. But, if the Dragon finds evidence that you can't keep a small commitment to yourself, it will burn up your dream before you even get out of the gate.

Fortunately, in Kathrine's case, following the advice from her dad satisfied the Dreamer and the Dragon. She collected evidence for her success through the simple practice of running a mile a day. Taking this inspired action transformed her and put her on a path toward a remarkable legacy. She went on to revolutionize the world of sports for women, all the way to the Olympic level. Kathrine Switzer is a Force at Work, positively influencing the lives of millions of aspiring female athletes from around the world.

Adopt Purposeful Practices

Purposeful practices like Kathrine's "running a mile a day" begin with a simple desire. Remember, there is no need to justify or question what your particular desire is. Trust that it has been given to you, and trust the process to reveal more as you follow it.

EXAMPLES OF PURPOSEFUL PRACTICES

A purposeful practice is a specific agreement you make with yourself that moves you closer to something you really want. It serves as evidence of your commitment to your Dreamer and your Dragon. Remember, smaller is better!

- Run a mile a day.
- Write for two hours every week.
- Initiate a conversation with one stranger every week.
- Journal three pages every morning.
- Walk in nature for twenty minutes each day.
- Serve at a Care Center every week.
- Begin the day with a 10-minute meditation.
- Spend 20 minutes each day practicing Spanish.

My friend Laurie Chandler wanted to be a writer. She had a desire to write Art Déco fiction. You can always tell an authentic desire by how specific and unique it is to each person. I was surprised to learn Art Déco fiction has its own genre!

Laurie was married, living in New York City, working part-time, and raising two small boys. She knew that more than 80 percent of Americans shared her desire to write a book and that only about 2 percent ever would.[26] The odds were stacked against her.

She took on a purposeful writing practice by committing to writing for two hours every week. For the next several years, you could find Laurie at the Starbucks on East 80th and Second Avenue every Saturday morning. Week after week, she walked to that Starbucks, put her butt in the seat, and wrote for two hours. Along the way, she learned first-hand the benefits of engaging in the creative process with discipline. She also saw how this practice positively impacted every area of her life. Desiring to share this insight with others, she first wrote a book called *Keeping Creativity Alive*. This book wasn't the original book she planned on writing, but it was an important step on the way to her bigger dream. I'll never forget the day she called me to share she had just received a three-year book deal from Kensington Publishers for her Art Déco mystery series about the adventures of Lane Sanders, a savvy heroine solving mysteries in the dazzling world of New York City in the 1930s. The first book is called *The Silver Gun* by L.A. Chandler. Check it out!

The power of purposeful practice is available to all of us. No matter your age or circumstance, a purposeful practice is the first step to unlocking a new chapter in your life.

Three Keys to a Powerful Purposeful Practice

These three elements make up an effective purposeful practice:

1. **Connect your practice to who you are becoming.** The difference between a habit and a purposeful practice is like the difference between a goal and an intention. You can't do a purposeful practice mindlessly. Your practice is a confident expression of your desire, and by practicing it, you are aligning your physical body with your internal intention and thus transforming your identity. Running a mile a day turned Kathrine

into a runner. At that Starbucks in New York City, Laurie became a writer.

2. **Keep your practice small.** Think of it as pass or fail. In this case, the size and scope of the action doesn't matter as much as whether you check the box. Remember, your brain is looking for evidence that you will do what you say you will do. As you grow in your practice, you will take bigger steps. But when you begin, make your purposeful practice the biggest step you can take with a 100 percent completion rate. Go for a walk, do one squat, write for 10 minutes, make one sales call a day. With a purposeful practice, you don't need a touchdown, but you do need a lot of first downs!

3. **Make your practice a high priority.** The main goal of the purposeful practice is to restore integrity with yourself and get your Dreamer and your Dragon on the same page. To unleash these forces, make the agreement a non-negotiable part of your day. Whatever you pick, let it be a level-five commitment — then do whatever it takes to make it happen.

Exercise Is a Great Building Block

Anytime you set a goal, only two things can stop you: your own internal limiting beliefs or external obstacles. A professional coach will help you identify and overcome them both. You address limiting beliefs by becoming aware of them, challenging them, and replacing them. External obstacles require awareness and strategy. One of the best ways to build the resilience you will need in both areas is a purposeful practice of daily exercise.

When I became a new coach, one of the first priorities I set was a commitment to my personal health. I included a workout as part of my workday. I treated this purposeful practice as any other appointment I would schedule with a client.

This discipline had multiple benefits. Exercise became the building block of my ability to make and keep agreements with myself. The activity released endorphins and put me in a more positive mental state. I demonstrated agency with my schedule by working out in the middle of the day when the gym was nearly empty. Completing my workout in the early afternoon hours after the lunch crowd returned to their desks empowered me and reminded me I could zig when others zagged. This practice connected me with the intention and vision I had of becoming a successful and sought-after coach.

Daily stretching, yoga, or walking are great purposeful practices with which to start. Keep it easy and doable. This gets us around the modern-day myth that we need to find motivation before we begin. Steve Chandler eloquently states the obvious, "What needs to occur is the walking, not the motivation to walk."[27]

Exercise became the building block of my ability to make and keep agreements with myself.

Here are a few more examples of purposeful practices for you to consider.

1. One of my clients chose "Brave" as her One Word for the year. To support her intention, she created a purposeful practice of doing one small act of bravery every day and kept a record of those acts in her journal.

2. Another client, who wanted to jump to another career track, started a purposeful practice of leaving her demanding remote job for thirty minutes every day to go for a walk over lunch. This purposeful practice reconnected her with nature and allowed her to see how out of control her current job was. It was the first step she took to create space and establish agency over her schedule. Though a seemingly small step, it fell like the first of many dominoes, setting her on a completely different trajectory in her personal life and in her career. Never underestimate the power of honoring a small desire when paired with the commitment of a purposeful practice.

3. Almost every day, I enjoy a leisurely, extended afternoon walk. Sometimes I listen to an audiobook. Walking in the woods and listening to authors who are expanding our collective consciousness elevates my thinking, and I begin to see a place for my ideas and concepts in the world, too. Through this practice, I feel as though I am becoming more of a thought leader. Plus, walking regulates and calms me. It is often the highlight of my day.

When it comes to your practice, remember to dream big but to start small. In no time, you will begin to experience the transformational power of your purposeful practice.

Reflection

What purposeful practices would help you feel more aligned with your purpose and your vision? Find the Purposeful Practice Tracker in your *Forces at Work Guidebook* and track your progress for a month. Feel free to adjust the practices at the beginning of each week until you find the ones that resonate with you.

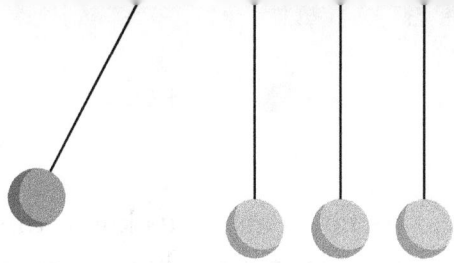

CHAPTER 14

find purposeful projects

"Don't let what you can't do keep you from doing what you can."

— Unknown

The second form of inspired action is a purposeful project. You can view a purposeful project as an experiment.

I met George outside the subway stop at Harvard when I was visiting the campus this summer. In a crowd of hurried students and parents, he stood out because he was sitting in a red camp chair with a built-in shaded top and a sign on top that simply said, "I give free advice." He wore a ball cap in primary colors with a small propeller on top and a T-shirt that said, "Free Advice Offered and Accepted — No Politics or Religion."

The number of strangers lined up to talk to him surprised me, and his interactions with people painted a profoundly moving scene. I found myself stepping into the line.

As far as any of us knew, this guy had no credentials or experience to offer, but no one seemed to care. George listened more than he talked, reminding me of the truth that being listened to feels so much like being loved that most people can't tell the difference.

The woman in front of me wiped tears from her eyes as he encouraged her to set boundaries with her adult daughter. When my turn came, I asked him why he did it. He said, "There is so much hatred, discord, sadness, and hurt in the world. People come and share their problems, and I do my best to help them." I wondered if he had a counseling or coaching background. He did not. George was a retired commercial real estate executive who had grown restless and wanted to do something that mattered. The realization that many people had to bear their burdens alone troubled him. He felt that if they just had someone to talk to, their load would feel lighter.

George decided he would be that someone. He created a simple project — an experiment — in which he regularly planted his chair in a public spot, put his sign up, and talked with strangers for hours at a time. "I mostly just listen," he said. "They feel better about getting it off their chests, and I feel better for helping them."

He shared with me how he'd figured out the logistics of his project. It was a simple setup, but it required a bit of thought. I noticed the four orange cones surrounding his chair, keeping people from tripping over him. A small duffle bag containing a few personal items rested beside him. George had spent time researching local ordinances to see if he'd need a permit. After experimenting with a few locations, he decided he liked the Harvard spot best.

George is positively impacting lives with his project. More importantly, listening to the struggles and frustrations of strangers from diverse backgrounds is transforming *him*. As a result, his purpose is expanding, too. George and I have been keeping in touch. He plans to write a book about this experience, and there is a one-man play in the works as well.

As I stepped away so the next person could have their turn, George gave me a small sticker imprinted with a caricature of himself and the words, "I got free advice from George." I keep it inside my notebook, and it still brings a smile whenever I see it.

George is a Force at Work.

The Buried Life Project

As I mentioned, my word for 2022 was "Elevate." One way I wanted to Elevate was by surrounding myself with big thinkers, visionaries, and creatives, who would inspire and help me grow.

One of my favorite non-profit clients holds a large community breakfast as a fundraiser. I love supporting these events, and since it was several hours away and would be an early morning call, I went up the night before and stayed at the Vera Bradley Hotel.

The night before the breakfast, I had dinner with my client, who was hosting the event. She understandably had her hands full with details for the morning. We realized Ben Nemtin, the guest speaker they had chosen for the event, was staying at the Vera Bradley, too. Having many details to attend to, my client asked if I might be willing to drive Ben to the event in the morning since I'd be coming anyway. I already know a little about Ben, and I was delighted to have some extra time with him.

Ben has an extraordinary story and is inspiring people around the world to create and complete a bucket list of things they want to do before they die. I wasn't surprised to learn his inspirational work also began as a project.

Ben was a college dropout who struggled with debilitating depression. During this time, a small group of friends surrounded him and lovingly forced him out of his self-imposed isolation. In fact, each of them was grappling with his own personal challenges, so they began looking for ways to support each other. They came up with an idea to create a bucket list of 100 things they wanted to do before they died. As the idea came to life, they decided it would be fun to film themselves completing items on the list.

So, armed with their list, a camera, and a sense of adventure, they set off in a borrowed RV on a two-week project to complete as many items on their list as they could.

"In the beginning," they wrote, "we put items on the list just for a laugh. We pretended we were unstoppable and wrote down whatever popped into our heads."[28] They documented their experiment on social media and soon had a growing following. Early in the project, they decided that for every item they crossed off their list, they would help fulfill a stranger's bucket list item, too.

This created a movement as an army of strangers started pitching in to help them knock out their list. As a result, they've accomplished incredible things, like "#95: Play Basketball with Obama," "#74: Help Deliver a Baby," "#124: Be on Oprah," "#2: Lead a Parade," and "#53:

Make a Television Show." You can find the full list at theburiedlife.com.[29] They only have a handful of items left on their list. One of them is "#100: Go to Space." (I need to introduce Ben to Anousheh Ansari!)

The two-week project has continued for over ten years. When the four young men started, they couldn't fully articulate the project. They just stepped into action. "What we shared was just a feeling. We moved forward without a plan."

Inspired action leaves room to explore and gives us permission to be playful. As Ben and his friends can attest, even small actions set big things in motion.

> Inspired action leaves room to explore and gives us permission to be playful.

"We stumbled on the idea of creating a bucket list at a young age, and it has slowly evolved into a lifestyle of intention," says Ben. "We failed a lot. But when we succeeded, I noticed there were patterns of things we did again and again and again."

Today, Ben speaks worldwide and inspires people, young and old, to check off items on their bucket lists.

"This is the new leadership," he says. "By putting yourself first, you put yourself in a position to help others."

I agree. Too many teachers and consultants end up teaching theory, not sharing real experiences, and leadership becomes hypothetical. This is why purposeful projects are so important. Ben discovered what my friend Neil Gordon shared with me years ago: "People don't change because of what they know to be true, but because of what they believe to be possible."

Ben's project led to a unique and important purpose for his life that is impacting the world in powerful ways. He and his friends worked hard to build The Buried Life, but they also had a blast doing it.

Projects Expand Your Purpose

One of my clients, Mady Stazzone, also found her true purpose through a project. Mady and her husband are both physicians. At the request of two local surgeons, they visited a hospital in the Dominican Republic. They were shocked at the conditions they saw.

Mady had almost refused to go on the trip. Not only was she afraid of exotic bugs, but she was also raising four children and had many other responsibilities on her place. But an internal voice urged her to go.

While there, she met a young patient who eventually died from infection after an unsuccessful surgery to correct his severe scoliosis. Deeply touched by his story, Mady recognized that patients were dying for lack of education and training for the nurses. She also realized she knew how to help.

For the last 12 years, she and Enrico, along with their friend, who is an anesthesiologist, have returned to the Dominican Republic every year with a team to provide lifesaving surgeries, education, and equipment for the hospital. Their organization, The Pediatric Orthopedic Project, is responsible for over 500 lifesaving surgeries. Making the most of every resource, Mady organized the surgery recipients into a volunteer army. As the patients heal, they return to help the new patients with their physical therapy. Mady continues to research better ways to help her patients. Recently Mady and Enrico were granted a patent for a process they were instrumental in developing — one that has healed spinal cord injuries once believed to be permanent. The implications for the world are promising!

Mady and Enrico Stazzone are Forces at Work.

I hope you can see there are a million ways to create a purposeful project and only one way not to — and that is by doing nothing. Instead, why not create a project of your own?

One Door Opens Another

Purposeful projects can open many doors you have never imagined walking through — often by leading to new purposeful projects.

For example, writing *Forces at Work* is a purposeful project that also sparked several other projects for me. During my research phase, the phrase "spill the wind" captured my curiosity. I chose a fun inspired (and inspiring!) action by booking the sailing experience on the *Mary Day*, which became an important chapter in this book.

Another project emerged for me as I revisited some of my long-held desires. I love theater, and this year, the Universe conspired for me to invest in two productions I believe are Broadway bound.

This didn't occur by chance. Seven years ago, I made a rather impulsive decision to sell the home we'd lived in for 12 years and move into a more affluent neighborhood nearby. It was an intuitive decision. I was being guided, and everything that needed to happen for our move fell into place effortlessly.

The first weekend we were in our new house, I met Sam Arce, who turned out to be our new neighbor three doors down. Over time, our families have become like family to each other, sharing holidays and vacations, hosting fund-raisers, and walking through hardships together.

When we met, Sam was just beginning his journey as a Broadway producer. Today, he has many credits to his name. Learning about my passion for Broadway, he created a place for me on his investment team. It has been an exciting and exhilarating ride.

We recently traveled to London for the opening of my first project as an investor: *Mandela*, the musical. There, I met the other producers, the creative team, and the cast. Sam directed me to this particular project because we both recognized Nelson Mandela as a Force at Work — an ordinary person who acted in alignment with purpose and made a far-reaching positive impact on the world. It was a perfect project for me. While in London, I met Nelson Mandela's granddaughter, Nandi Mandela, and her son, Luvuyo Madasa. I am overjoyed to partner with them in bringing this important story to the world stage.

One project often leads to another. I reconnected with another producer friend, Melissa Jones, who happened to be in London at the same time. Melissa invited me to a workshop for *SuperYou*, her latest passion project. Melissa is a Tony-nominated producer whose projects include *Come from Away* and *Jagged Little Pill*. At the London workshop,

I immediately saw how the *SuperYou* project connected to my purpose of helping people fulfill their potential and overcome their limiting beliefs and obstacles. Even as I watched the actors perform without costumes or a set, I could envision how the production would come to life. I gratefully accepted the invitation to invest in this project as well. Ironically, I had introduced Melissa to Sam a few years earlier, and Sam is taking on the co-producing role with *SuperYou*.

On my vision board last year was a desire to travel internationally for my work. I'll likely be returning to London in the Fall of 2023 for the opening of *SuperYou* and, hopefully, the premier of *Mandela* on the West End.

My projects have grown with me. I didn't begin by investing thousands of dollars in international projects. In my coaching practice, one of my early projects was to create a workbook for my clients. That project has evolved into this book and into the *Forces at Work Guidebook*.

Are your wheels turning? What purposeful projects are percolating in you? Here are some guidelines as you begin.

Getting Started With Your Purposeful Project

1. Brainstorm three to five potential projects.
2. Use the Commitment Scale found in chapter 12 to determine which one to begin first.
3. Imagine your outcome. What do you hope will happen as a result of completing this project?
4. Take the first step!

The EAT Project

Another valuable, though much different, project is the EAT Project, which stands for Eliminate All Tolerations.

New endeavors require time and energy. This 30-day project can help you free up some space.

A toleration is unfinished or old business. It could be the group you still attend only because you made a commitment and don't want to disappoint someone. Your list of tolerations may include a cluttered closet, a dripping faucet, a lack of personal

> A toleration is anything taking your energy but no longer fulfilling a meaningful purpose.

time, a lack of quality time with the kids, ill-fitting clothes, a lack of vacation plans, unused subscriptions. It might be maintenance for your home or your car, promises you have yet to keep, unfinished arguments, or unspoken truths. A toleration is anything taking your energy but no longer fulfilling a meaningful purpose.

Tolerations are like drafty windows in an old house. You can keep turning up the heat, but until you seal the leaks or replace the windows, you are wasting energy.

ELIMINATE ALL TOLERATIONS: INSTRUCTIONS

To complete your first toleration project, just follow these guidelines.

1. Create your list. This is your master list of grievances. Write down everything that bugs you or drains your energy. Don't rationalize or explain; just get it all out on paper.

Keep the list with you for three days and add things as they come to you. The flood will slow to a trickle as you empty them all out onto the page. For most of my clients, this is a cathartic experience, although for some, it can be overwhelming. Remember the J-Curve effect? When we step out of denial, things can seem harder for a short time. Keep going!

2. Evaluate your list. After you go a day or so without adding many more new items, go through the list, and next to each item, write what it would take to resolve it. No commitment of action is necessary at this point; just decide what action step would be required to resolve the toleration — "clean out the closet," "call a plumber," "box up old clothes," "resign from the board," "quit my job."

3. Eliminate items. For the next 30 days, take easy, fun, doable steps to see how many items you can eliminate. Address one category at a time to close the leaks and open your creative energy.

4. Don't make new any new commitments during this period. During this time, resist the urge to add any new commitments to your schedule unless they absolutely delight you.

Reflection

What project will you create as an expression of your purpose? Could you listen like George or inspire like Ben? Who are your "ride or die" friends who could partner with you?

As you work through the exercises in this chapter, don't forget to use the Project Planner and the EAT project worksheet available in your *Forces at Work Guidebook*.

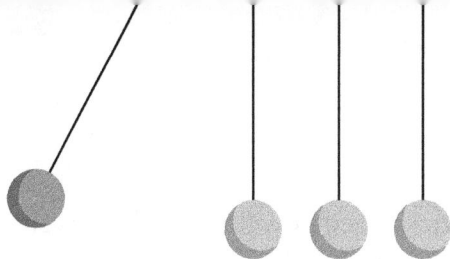

CHAPTER 15

invite powerful partnerships

"This is the Way"

— Din Djarin

You Need Some New Friends

A few years ago, I worked with a client we'll call Nancy. She was a former hospital executive who was building her own healthcare consulting business. She came to me because she recognized she had an opportunity to align her new endeavor with her highest and best purpose, and she wanted to make the most of it.

We began with the building blocks of *Forces at Work*. When we got to the inspired action step, Nancy changed her diet and started exercising.

A few months later, it was clear she had lost weight. She looked trim and fit and was positively glowing. She excitedly described how it seemed the weight was just dropping off. This didn't surprise me; her body was aligning with the vision of who she really wanted to be and how she intended to show up.

But then her countenance dimmed as she described a puzzling encounter with some of her closest friends the week before.

Nancy and this group of friends regularly met for dinner. The others noticed the physical changes in Nancy's appearance. As she excitedly shared about the new direction she'd found for her life and business, they grew quiet. Then, instead of celebrating her transformation, they criticized her and told her they thought she was "taking things a little too far." Can you imagine? This woman lost her extra weight as a side effect of aligning her life with purpose, and her dinner pals pushed back because it made them uncomfortable when she ordered a salad!

Unfortunately, I see responses like this all too often. Not everyone is ready to throw off a status quo lifestyle to become a Force at Work. Your positive changes disrupt their comfy ecosystems by providing evidence that something better is possible and what they are experiencing is *not* "just the way things are." Like a flashlight, Nancy's physical appearance illuminated her changing life but also shone a light on their lives, too. Of course, her friends were not intentionally sabotaging her, only expressing their non-conscious, fear-based response to change.

"You're going to need some new friends," I said simply.

I wasn't suggesting Nancy throw out her current relationships, and I am not implying this for you, either. I am merely suggesting you view them through the lens of who you want to be and evaluate whether your interactions with them bring you closer to or further from your vision. Then, set boundaries to protect the work you are doing for yourself.

I view Nancy's friends with compassion. I think they may eventually allow her choices to inspire them. But for now, Nancy needs some new friends who will celebrate and encourage her to keep moving forward.

When you embark on a new path, wonderful new partnerships will present themselves. Your new relationships may threaten those who are not secure in their own purpose and agency.

> When you embark on a new path, wonderful new partnerships will present themselves.

This can be especially true in family relationships, in which our family members may have put us in a box based on a role we played as we grew up. Sometimes, when we transform, the people who knew us before will still see us the same. We can approach them with empathy and understanding without allowing their reaction to alter our course.

Once, I worked with an attorney who admittedly had developed an Eeyore complex — you know, the character in *Winnie the Pooh* who is constantly grumpy and unhappy? Through our work, he began to recognize his cynical and sarcastic attitude no longer served him. He saw what it was costing him to maintain a pessimistic, glass-half-empty, victim-oriented persona. It manifested in overeating and entertaining himself to distract from the pain of misalignment and missed potential. As we walked through the Forces at Work steps, I saw glimmers of his true self, moments of brilliance and excitement. He had a unique and impressive dream — one I could easily see him stepping into. He was at the precipice of trading in his oars and learning to sail.

But he didn't. During one session, our work ended abruptly when he said, "Look, if I turn into a positive, uplifting kind of guy, my friends aren't going to buy it. They won't accept this new version of me."

We will never know. Maybe they would have given him a hard time, or maybe he didn't give them enough credit. Perhaps his bold changes would have disrupted their status quo and inspired them to change, too. Either way, he settled back into his old routine and let his dream gather dust on a shelf.

This is by far the most disappointing aspect of my job. I hate to see someone with so much potential give up on their dream and settle back into an old pattern. This is one of the main reasons I am creating the Forces at Work community. We all need a place to incubate our dreams. We need fellow travelers who are on similar paths and who can encourage and celebrate us as we create new habits and take brave steps to embrace our dreams.

Alignment Clears the Path to New Relationships

The good news? You are ready to connect with other Forces at Work in your community and in the world.

When you align your life with purpose, vision, agency, intention, and action, these inspired connections will happen. You don't need to force them. You only need to create space, be open to recognizing them, and step into the opportunities as they arise.

Rumi says, "What you seek is seeking you." Support is drawn to purpose. I believe the people you are looking for are also looking for you.

When I first decided to leave direct sales and become a full-time coach, I struggled to jump the track. All my income, expertise, and relationships were tied to my current reality. Like the example of the teeter-totter with two baskets on it, I would never move unless I started moving apples from my Current Reality basket into the Compelling Vision basket.

Until then, I'd only participated in industry conferences — that was my Current Reality basket. But when an opportunity presented itself, I decided to skip my own industry event and attend a local goal-setting workshop instead. With that inspired action, I put energy into my Compelling Vision basket.

That day, I showed up at a very large ballroom with hundreds of people eagerly waiting for the program to begin. As the speaker took the stage, I was transfixed. His name was CJ McClanahan. A gifted speaker, he told vivid stories, had us laughing, and skillfully delivered a fun and engaging presentation. The material he shared wasn't new to me. I had presented similar content for women in my industry many times. But it was a huge eye-opener to see him do this for the business community at large and see them eating it up. I instantly liked him and wondered if he would have any interest in talking with me.

The next week, I called his office and asked for an appointment. I didn't hear back right away, but I persisted. Finally, CJ agreed to meet me.

During that meeting, we instantly connected on matters of purpose, vision, family, and faith. I shared a little of my background, and he shared how he had been looking for someone to run one of his programs. Without having everything ironed out, he invited me to work with him.

CJ and I took some time to figure out exactly how our partnership would work. Eventually, he hired me to be his personal coach. When an extra office opened in his suite, he offered to rent it to me. Over the years, he referred countless clients to me and offered my name anytime he was double-booked for a speaking engagement. A few years after we met, we co-hosted his annual goal-setting workshop together, and it remains one of the highlights of my career. More importantly, CJ has become one of my dearest friends and most trusted colleagues. I don't like to imagine where I would be if I hadn't reached out and he hadn't agreed to meet me that day.

CJ and I partner together successfully because we share values and a vision to make our corner of the world a better place. Our partnership isn't transactional or competitive; it is collaborative. Because we truly care about each other's success, we accept feedback and listen to each other's challenges without judgment. CJ helps me see things I struggle to see in myself. At times, he believes more in my capabilities as a coach than I do. His confidence in me has been one of the greatest gifts I've ever received. Together, we've connected and collaborated to help our clients, made important introductions for them, and assisted many other leaders in taking the next steps in their purposeful projects.

Find the Mentors You May Never Meet

As a child, I began a lifelong love affair with reading. The local public library was within walking distance of my home. I loved the smell of print and new carpet and the gentle scent of the librarian's perfume enveloping me as I walked in. I would take the stairs to the children's section in the basement, grab a few books off the shelf, and settle into my favorite beanbag chair.

For many years, it was my sanctuary — heated in winter, air-conditioned in summer, and always safe, quiet, and peaceful. The library supplied an endless number of stories to keep me entertained, and it was free.

I read Nancy Drew, Trixie Belden, and the Hardy Boys. Judy Bloom taught me about life, and CS Lewis took me on a magical journey through a wardrobe. I won the summer reading contest three years in a row. Through reading, I traveled the world and met people who still influence and inspire me today.

> Through reading, I traveled the world and met people who still influence and inspire me today.

I still find most of my mentors in books. Most of them I will never meet, and yet they have profoundly influenced my life. Delightfully, in authoring my own book, I have met several of them in person. This was one of my deeper personal goals in writing and publishing a book — I wanted to join the community of authors who have had a profound impact on my life.

Meet Your Mentors When You Can

One of the mentors I've met in person is Gina DeVee. But before we ever met in person, the words in her book guided me through a challenging time in my career.

Shortly before the pandemic, I took a full-time job doing business development for one of my clients. Though I was a little wary of an eight-to-five commitment, I was drawn to the purpose-driven work, and being on an energetic and dedicated team excited me. Giving up some freedom and flexibility for some esprit de corps felt like a good trade-off.

But the pandemic quickly changed the entire landscape. Our company relied on in-person events, and scrambling into the virtual world took time. I felt helpless trying to sell something we hadn't fully defined. Companies were not signing new agreements amid so much global uncertainty. I struggled with a new routine that included a daily stand-up meeting. Endless video calls left me drained and frustrated.

During this time, I came across Gina's book, *The Audacity to Be Queen*.[30] Listening to her voice as I went on long walks in the afternoon awakened me. I knew I had to leave the job. Whatever I had hoped it would be, it wasn't good for me now. I also suspected my salary was a burden to the organization, and they needed to redirect those funds to a coordinated marketing effort and new programming.

I worried about disappointing a team I cared about, and I also worried about replacing the lost income. It didn't seem like a great time for me to go looking for new clients. But Gina's inspired words gave me the courage to trust my intuition and resign. The relief that followed gave a clear indicator that it was the right decision. Even though we'd never met, Gina was my mentor during this season, a calm, spiritual voice that I needed to help me navigate significant issues in my personal and professional life.

A year later, Gina hosted a small retreat, and I jumped at the opportunity to meet her. I was delighted to find she was the same in person as the woman I met in her book. We have since become friends, and I continue to learn and grow through her friendship.

As I close this final chapter, I want to share how you can cultivate powerful partnerships.

Collaborate; Don't Compete

Competitive people wear me out. I don't have a lot of energy for social climbers and one-uppers. I'm also done with transactional, quid pro quo relationships. Aren't you? I don't want to keep score anymore. These days, I look for grateful, generous givers who have freed themselves from the scarcity mindset and are ready to stretch to their full potential. They eagerly participate in the virtuous cycle because they have seen how it brings joy and fulfillment to their lives and the lives of others.

As an intention, I once chose "Generous" as my One Word for the year. I lived it out by saying yes whenever I was asked to give money. Though I didn't advertise this or talk about it, that year, no matter who asked, I said yes. The first yes went to the Boy Scout next door, who sold me 12 ounces of stale popcorn for $25. With the next yes, I sponsored a golf outing for an organization supporting kids in foster care. I even started keeping cash with me for the homeless man next to the ramp on the interstate (please don't @ me over this). My answer was yes, and I gave whatever I could. Not only did I elevate my money story that year, but I also attracted a new mentor friend who would help me grow an abundance mindset.

Ellen Rogin is the *New York Times* bestselling co-author of *Picture Your Prosperity*.[31] She came to town to speak for a women's organization where I served as an advisor. We stayed in touch and have become friends. She most recently attended my Forces at Work retreat, and now we are looking into more ways we can work together. What I admire about Ellen is that despite her success, she never shows a trace of competition. Her abundance mindset inspires me, and she is always up for an adventure. I can't wait to see what we will create together.

Even though I've never met most of my mentor authors in person, I still love introducing them to you. You'll find a list of extraordinary authors in the acknowledgement section at the back of this book. I hope you'll let them become your mentors, too!

Find Fun People

People who take themselves too seriously also wear me out. It's the rowing thing again. If they need to be a martyr, I can respect this season for them, but I know they are not a good partner for me right now. I like working with fun people who are aligned and ready to sail!

I just brought on a new partner to help me with my retreats. Brooke is the former client who named her Dragon Alice. She is competent and capable for sure, but do you know what she had over anyone else I considered for the position? It was the ability to make me laugh by knowing the words to every rap song that comes on. Life is too short to work with overly serious people!

In my opinion, your capacity for fun is a great indicator of your faith and maturity. It means you can do your part and trust the process to take you where you need to go. CJ is fun. Brooke is fun, and Ellen is fun. If I partner with them on any project, I know remarkable things will happen in the world, and we'll have fun doing it. We understand there are real and serious problems in the world, but that we are only responsible for our own part, and we can do our work and enjoy our lives at the same time.

> In my opinion, your capacity for fun is a great indicator of your faith and maturity.

Trust Your Gut

Finally, the best indicator of a good partnership is your inner voice. Trust your gut. How do you feel when you are around this person? Do you genuinely like, trust, and respect them? Are you able to make and keep clear agreements with them, and do you genuinely look forward to spending time with them? Are they doing something important in their communities? If yes, have a conversation and see how you can come alongside and learn from them. Even better, use your inspired imagination to come up with a project that seems fun to both of you, and step into action! Purpose attracts support.

Make a list of people you like, trust, and respect. Who are your mentors, and what gifts or lessons have they shared with you? Who else would you like to meet in person? It might be someone in your profession or someone you admire in the community. You could start by inviting them for coffee and ask them to share their story with you. Forces at Work find each other by taking the initiative to forge new connections. Of course, you are invited to connect with my community in the Forces at Work Facebook Group.

> Forces at Work find each other by taking the initiative to forge new connections.

Reflection

Who in your life supports and encourages you? Who do you suspect needs you to keep playing small to feel comfortable around you? Who are the mentors, authors, and leaders you admire? How can you connect with them or strengthen their positive influence in your life?

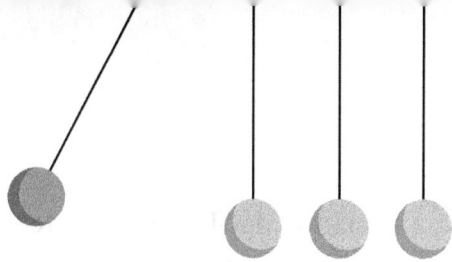

CHAPTER 16

you are a force at work

E very great story has an endearing hero who wants something, and a guide who helps them get it.

In the best stories, we cheer for a character who has an awakening and decides to chase their dream.

We become invested in their outcome, sharing their hopes and their disappointments. At the end, not only do we celebrate their victory, but we also celebrate their personal transformation.

This is my hope for you as you finish reading *Forces at Work*.

You are the hero of your story, and you are the one called to take action to move the story forward. Thank you for reading *Forces at Work* and for allowing me to play the role of your guide. I want to offer you one last exercise to guide you in awakening the Forces at Work within you.

Each morning when I wake, I journal my answers to a series of questions shared by Gabby Bernstein in her book *Super Attractor*.[32] Here is a recent entry in my journal:

1. How do I want to feel today? *Grateful. Relaxed. Confident. Joyful.*
2. Who do I want to be today? *The Lady who Knows that God is Gracious.* (This is the meaning of my name, and I love affirming this in my daily reflection!)
3. What do I want to receive today? *Guidance. Clarity. Encouragement. Revenue.*
4. What do I want to give today? *Kindness. Hope. Insight. Love.*

For one month, keep a journal by your bed and answer these questions immediately upon awakening. I consider this daily exercise a personal practice, and it helps me consistently tap into each of the internal Forces at Work we've discussed in this book.

Friend, success will find you if you begin with your purpose, create a compelling vision, establish your agency, connect with intention, and move into action. When you awaken and align the Forces at Work within, you become a powerful and compelling Force at Work in the world.

Yet, none of us do this alone. A cast of characters will enter your story and help shape your journey. I'd love to be a character in your story, and I hope one day we can meet in person!

> When you awaken and align the Forces at Work within, you become a powerful and compelling Force at Work in the world.

Someone told me if I wrote this book, the impact on me personally would overshadow any other outcomes. I can see this is true.

Bob Goff invited me to attend the writer's workshop he hosts at a beautiful retreat center called the Oaks, just outside of San Diego. I accepted his invitation, and the workshop crystallized some of the changes that took place in me while I was writing.

What has become clear for me is a renewed desire to help others who have experienced childhood trauma. It is a global-sized problem, and I know I want to have a bigger impact than what I can do alone. Will you join me?

I partner with three organizations that are helping vulnerable kids. I hope you will take a few minutes to visit their websites and consider getting involved, too. The children we serve will grow up to reflect the care and love they receive today. Each founder is a personal friend and a Force at Work.

(Please practice due diligence and vet any organization before you give financially. I have done so with all three of these and am confident my money is doing exactly as I intend.)

Pediatric Orthopedic Project — pophopeteam.org

Hands of Hope — handsofhopein.org

SuperYou Foundation — superyoufun.org

Thank you for reading my very first book! I hope you continue on your journey to become a Force at Work. I would love to hear from you. You can reach me at missy@missyshopshire.com

A FEW MINUTES COULD MEAN A LOT

If this book has helped you, and you would like to share the message, please consider writing a positive review on Amazon. This small act could have a big impact on the *Forces at Work* message reaching someone who needs it right now. Please accept my deepest thanks for helping spread this message by sharing a review!

acknowledgments

Thank you, Adam, for being my person for the last three decades and for the beauty of seeing things through.

Thank you, Alec, Jensen, Grace, Stanley, Jack, and Isla. You are my heart and my greatest purpose.

To my clients, past, present, and future! I would have nothing to offer in this book had you not invited me into your stories and allowed me the great privilege of walking with you as your coach. I am always in your corner and cheering for your success and happiness. You are changing the world, and it is pure joy for me to play a small role in that.

Thank you, Mary Kay Ash and all the directors and consultants who taught me about sisterhood and dreaming big. Special thanks to my mentor, Paula Light, and my long-time faithful assistant, Kara Jones.

Thank you, Mary, my coach for all these years. You met me where I was and opened doors of new possibilities for me.

Thank you, CJ. You are my enduring friend and trusted colleague. You helped me jump the tracks, and I will always be grateful.

Thank you, Sam, for always having my back and for allowing me to take part in bringing *Mandela* and *SuperYou* to the stage. And to Miya, Sammy, Michelle, and Waleed for sharing your family with mine.

Thank you to my big brother, Andy, for your big heart and ready support.

Thank you to the women who have supported and empowered me over the years, beginning with my mom, Oneta Nelson, my sisters, Becky and Denise, and my mother-in-law, Marti.

Thank you, Portland, my best friend and confidant. I found a treasure in you! And to Todd and the kids, thank you for sharing her with me and for often sharing your holidays with us.

Special thanks to Dianne and Tari, my angels. I'm so proud of how we've grown since middle school. You bring so much joy and laughter to my life.

Thank you, Stephanie; you are my small group!

Thank you, Marc and Alicia, for the fun, comfort, and wisdom you bring to our lives.

Thank you to the women in my mastermind groups over the years. You amaze and inspire me.

And finally, to the following authors who have influenced and shaped me by sharing your ideas and wisdom through your books. Together you've provided me with the most extraordinary education that has empowered me to live the life of my dreams. I have read and reread your books many times. I can't imagine where I would be without you.

- Lynn Twist, Ellen Rogin, and David Bach. You transformed my money story and showed me the riches of generosity.

- Michael Neill, Steve Chapman, and Tim Keller. You shaped my understanding of purpose, vision, and belief.

- Gina DeVee and Gabrielle Bernstein. Your strong feminine guidance instills calm and confidence in me, and you have renewed my connection with my Source.

- Marcia Weider for sharing Dream Coach with me and challenging me to put more energy into my dream than into my reality.

- Donald Miller and Bob Goff for showing me I could live a better story and for being even more awesome in person than you are online.

- Anousheh Ansari, Kathrine Switzer, and Ben Nemptin for living extraordinary lives and leading the way for others to do the same.

Lastly, thank you to the team at Niche Pressworks for helping me wrangle this book into the world. Special thanks to my editor, Melanie Hahn-Greene, whose edits and suggestions I was delighted to accept over and over because they were always on point and insightful.

about missy

Missy Shopshire started her career in sales, reaching the top 2 percent in a multi-billion-dollar company. She held that position for over ten years, during which she learned the importance of building a team, leading them well, and working toward a shared vision of success. Even so, something was missing.

Then, two life-altering events caused her to reevaluate her life. Her four-year-old daughter fought — and won — a battle with stage 3 kidney cancer. Shortly after, Missy herself experienced a rare infection that left her in a coma fighting for her life.

As she recovered, Missy awakened to her inner voice and started making big changes in her life and career. Leaving the sales industry at the top of her game, she switched gears to become a certified life and business coach. Now, she helps leaders do what she learned to do —align with a higher purpose and achieve their true potential.

By sharing this passionate message of purpose and belief through coaching and speaking, Missy is on a mission to help leaders embrace their circumstances, step into their deepest-held dreams and desires, and become Forces at Work.

Work with me!

Are you ready for more?

Visit my website to learn how you can work with me as a coach or speaker.

I support executives, entreprenuers, and teams who have big dreams and are ready to become Forces at Work! Learn more at www.missyshopshire.com or email me at missy@missyshopshire.com

endnotes

1   Lynne Twist, *The Soul of Money: Transforming Your Relationship with Money and Life* (New York: W. W. Norton & Company, Inc., 2003).

2   Lynne Twist, *The Soul of Money*, pp. 49–50.

3   Melody Beattie, *The Language of Letting Go* (Center City, MN: Hazelden Foundation, 1990), p. 320.

4   Taylor Protocols, "The Core Values Index (CVI) Is More than an Assessment of Personality," accessed March 30, 2023, https://www.taylorprotocols.com/CVI-Home.

5   Definitions taken directly from https://www.taylorprotocols.com; used with permission.

6   Anousheh Ansari and Homer Hickam, *My Dream of Stars: From Daughter of Iran to Space Pioneer* (New York: Palgrave MacMillan, 2010).

7   Anousheh Ansari, "Only as Much as We Dream Can We Be," TED Talks, February 6, 2017, https://www.youtube.com/watch?v=fa4Ure_-5l4.

8   Viktor E. Frankl, *Man's Search for Meaning* (London: Rider, 2004).

9   Wikipedia, "Viktor Frankl," accessed February 24, 2023, https://en.wikipedia.org/wiki/Viktor_Frankl.

10 Jack Canfield and Janet Switzer, *The Success Principles 10th Anniversary Edition: How to Get from Where*

You Are to Where You Want to Be (New York: Harper Collins, 2015).

11 Joe Dispenza, *Breaking the Habit of Being Yourself* (Carlsbad, CA: Hay House, 2013), p. 47.

12 Michael Neill, *You Can Have What You Want* (Carlsbad, CA: Hay House, Inc., 2006).

13 Bob Goff, *Love Does, Discover a Secretly Incredible Life in an Ordinary World*, Nashville, TN: Thomas Nelson Publishing, 2012).

14 Love Does, "About Us," accessed February 24, 2023, https://lovedoes.org/our-story/.

15 Ian V. Rowe, *Agency* (West Conshohocken, PA: Templeton Press, 2022), pp. 4–5.

16 Michael Neill, *You Can Have What You Want*, p. 139.

17 Cal Newport, *Deep Work* (New York: Hachette Book Group, 2016).

18 *Star Wars: Episode V, The Empire Strikes Back* (Lucasfilm, 1980).

19 Mary Lore, *Managing Thought: Think Differently. Think Powerfully. Achieve New Levels of Success* (New York: McGraw-Hill, 2010).

20 Byron Katie, *Loving What Is: Four Questions That Can Change Your Life* (New York: Three Rivers Press, 2002).

21 Lynn Twist, *The Soul of Money.*

22 Saul Mcleod, PhD, "Maslow's Hierarchy of Needs," Simply Psychology, April 4, 2022, https://www.simply-psychology.org/maslow.html.

23 Andrew Wallas, *Intention: How to Tap into the Most Underrated Power in the Universe* (London: Octopus Publishing Group Ltd., 2019), p 12.

24 Jon Gordan, Dan Britton, Jimmy Page, and Don Gordon, *One Word That Will Change Your Life, Expanded Edition* (Hoboken, NJ: Wiley, 2014).

25 Kathrine Switzer, *Marathon Woman* (Boston, MA: Da Capo Press, 2017), p.12.

26 Joseph Epstein, "Think You Have a Book in You? Think Again," September 28, 2002, *The New York Times*, https://www.nytimes.com/2002/09/28/opinion/think-you-have-a-book-in-you-think-again.html.

27 Steve Chandler, *The Life Coaching Connection* (Bandon, OR: Robert D Reed Publishers), p117.

28 Dave Lingwood, Ben Nemtin, Duncan Penn, and Jonnie Penn, *What Do You Want to Do Before You Die? Moving, Unexpected, and Inspiring Answers to Life's Most Important Question* (New York: Artisan, 2018).

29 The Buried Life, "The List," accessed March 18, 2023, (https://theburiedlife.com/the-list).

30 Gina DeVee, *The Audacity to Be Queen: The Unapologetic Art of Dreaming Big and Manifesting Your Most Fabulous Life* (New York: Hatchette Book Group, 2020).

31 Ellen Rogin and Lisa Kueng, *Picture Your Prosperity* (Northfield, IL: Two Tango Productions, 2021).

32 Gabrielle Bernstein, *Super Attractor* (Carlsbad, CA: Hay House, 2019), p. 199.

www.ingramcontent.com/pod-product-compliance
Lightning Source LLC
Chambersburg PA
CBHW071600210326
41597CB00019B/3337

* 9 7 8 1 9 5 2 6 5 4 8 0 0 *